AT THE AGE OF SEVENTY, the equivalent of an SAS back Camino – the Pilgrims' Walk terminating at the magnificen country's Galician capital, Santiago de Compostela.

This is the daily diary of her burden-laden 500-mile trek.

Packed with all the colourful characters, Christian values, spiritual and psychological enlightenment, savoury and unsavoury encounters and occurrences she experienced along the way, Maggie's tale is a 'must read' for all those with sensitivity and awareness who have ever harboured an unfulfilled desire to achieve something absurdly satisfying in later life.

This intrepid lady's mantra must surely have been - Just Do It!

*

About the Author

Maggie de Vos is married and lives in Sussex.

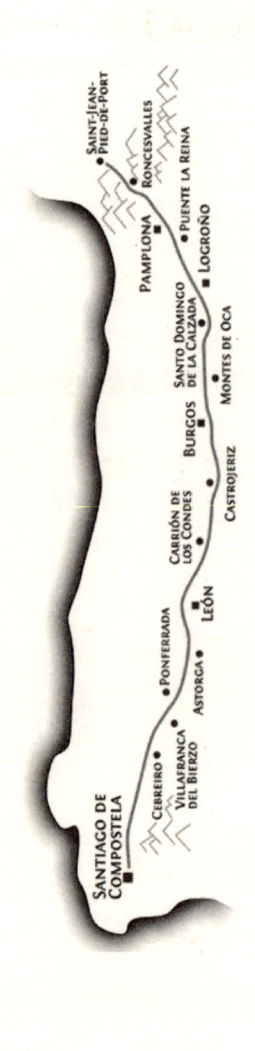

SANTIAGO AT SEVENTY

THE DIARY

OF

MY PILGRIMAGE

MAGGIE de VOS

Copyright

Maggie de Vos

©

Second Edition

2016

The author asserts the moral right under the Copyright, Designs and Patents Act 1988 to be identified as the author of this work.

All Rights reserved.

No part of this publication may be reproduced, stored in a retrieval system, or transmitted, in any form or by any means without the prior written consent of the author, nor be otherwise circulated in any form of binding or cover other than that in which it is published and without a similar condition being imposed on the subsequent purchaser.

ISBN: 9780993506406

Printed and bound in Great Britain by Clays Ltd, St Ives plc

British Library C.I.P.

A pilgrim (from the Latin peregrinus) is a traveler (literally one who has come from afar) who is on a journey to a holy place. Typically, this is a physical journey (often on foot) to some place of special significance to the adherent of a particular religious belief system. In the spiritual literature of Christianity, the concept of pilgrim and pilgrimage may refer to the experience of life in the world (considered as a period of exile) or to the inner path of the spiritual aspirant from a state of wretchedness to a state of beatitude.

This book is dedicated to pilgrims – everywhere . . . and to the memory of my dear mother who died too young and too early.

CONTENTS OF MY RUCKSACK

Anti histamine tablets
Bourneville chocolate
Bras (x 2)
Cagoul (waterproof)
Camera
Camping towel (bath size)
Coffee (instant, in individual packets)
Compeed plasters (in case of blisters)
Cosmetics – moisture cream, lipstick etc.
Credit cards (x 2)
Cutlery (knife, fork and spoon)
Diary
Dried fruit (apricots, cranberries, prunes & raisins)
Driving licence (why on earth?)
First aid kit (with bandages, Germoline antiseptic cream, plasters etc.)
Foot deodorant
Fleece pullover
Flip-flops (guard against catching verrucas and athlete's foot in the showers)
Glucosamine gel (for muscle pains)
Guide books (x2)
Hair band
Hand towel (proper terry towelling - not camping variety!)
Hat with cockle shell attached
Hot chocolate mix
Kendal mint cake
Knee straps (x 2)
Knickers (x 3)
Laxatives
Leggings (x 2)
New Testament

Nuts (shelled almonds & walnuts)
Oat biscuits
Panti liners (to save on knicker washing)
Passport
Pilgrim passport
Pins (2 dozen, babies' nappy-sized)
Plastic plate & cup
Poncho (waterproof, extra large size to cover rucksack as well as me)
Porridge (24 individual packets)
Pyjamas (silk, as protection from bed bugs)
Reading book (The Dancer - Rudolph Nureyev's biography)
Ryvita
Shoes (spare, as a relief from boots)
Shorts (x 2 prs)
Silk tops (x 2)
Sleeping-bag (with inner liner)
Sleeping pills
Swiss army knife (why on earth?)
Tea bags (36)
Toilet roll
Toothbrush (electric, with 2 spare batteries)
Torch
Trousers (x 2 prs)
Socks (x 3 prs)
String
Vaseline
Wet wipes
Whistles (x 2)
Yoga mat

NB. When I left Eastbourne my rucksack weighed 15 kilos. Even after giving away and losing countless items it still weighed 11.2 kilos at the airport on my way home.

CONTENTS PAGE

Prologue	page 13
The Beginning	page 17
Pamplona to Puente la Reina	page 23
Puente la Reina to Cirauqui	Page 29
Cirauqui to Viana	page 37
Viana to Navarrete	page 43
Navarrete to Najere	page 49
Najere to Viloria de Rioja	page 53
Viloria de Rioja to Villa Franca Montes de Oca	page 65
Villa Franca de Montes de Oca to Burgos	page 69
Burgos	page 71
Still in Burgos	page 75
Burgos to Villabilla de Burgos	page 79
Villabilla de Burgos to Hontanas	page 87
Hontanas to Fromista	page 93
Fromista to Carrion de los Condes	page 97

Carrion de los Condes to Sahagun	page 101
Sahagun to Leon	page 107
Leon	page 113
Leon to La Casa del Camino	page 119
La Casa del Camino to Santa Catalina de Somoza	page 123
Santa Catalina to El Acebo	page 127
El Acebo to Ponferrada	page 133
Ponferrada to Ruitelan	page 137
Ruitelan to Fonfria	page 145
Fonfria to Samos	page 155
Samos to Portomarin	page 161
Portomarin to Palas de Rei	page 165
Palas de Rei to Melide	page 171
Melide to Arzua	page 175
Arzua to Arca	page 177
Arca to Santiago de Compostela	page 181
Santiago de Compostela	page 185
To Finisterre	page 189

Epilogue   page 192

PROLOGUE

BARBATE - Costa de la Luz, Cadiz Province, Andalucia, in southern Spain . . . Semana Santa - 2010

IT IS A FULL YEAR SINCE I WALKED the Camino, the ancient pilgrim route across the north of Spain to Santiago de Compostela.
Now I feel ready to re-read the diary I kept along the way. Maybe now I can fully make sense of it and appreciate what drove me to it, why I had to go.
Why and how I did it.
Perhaps I can now assimilate what I discovered about myself: Maybe answer the question that the Camino poses to every pilgrim – Who are you?
It seems to me that I have always known about pilgrims. My mother had a copy of John Bunyan's The Pilgrim's Progress, its flysheet inscribed to:-
Meg Foster, School Prize 1927.
She treasured this book and when she died in 1949 I treasured it too. Sadly, I never managed to read it and somewhere over the years, to my shame and sorrow, the precious book was lost.

Some time ago I visited a friend in hospital. She passed me a copy of Pilgrim Snail by Ben Nimmo, 'You must read this,' she said, 'it is so heart warming and inspiring.'
It was, and is.
It tells of a young man who walked from Canterbury Cathedral in England to Santiago de Compostela in Spain in memory of a girl-friend who had died tragically young. His journey took nine months and along the way he raised money by busking with his trombone in bars and cafés.
When I finished reading it, for no logical reason, I made a secret promise to myself that one day I would walk the Camino.
I would walk to Santiago de Compostela.

Over the next several years life and living seemed to get in the way and I always managed to postpone undertaking the pilgrimage - until my 70th birthday loomed on the horizon, and I decided that my Camino had to be now or never.
I reasoned that if I told my family and friends that I was going to do a pilgrimage there would be no way for me to back out – I would have to do it – my pride would push me to it.
Some folks thought I was mad and tried to talk me out of it, while others just stood back in disbelief, but most were supportive and very encouraging.
I set my departure date – 25th March 2009 and started to make countless lists of things I would need to see me along the way.
I crossed off each of these items as I bought and stored them, and wrote new lists.
I joined the Confraternity of St. James - the UK-based charity established to promote the pilgrimage to the shrine of St James in Santiago, and attended their meetings in

London where I learned as much as I could of the do's, don'ts and pitfalls of walking the Camino.

For Christmas 2008 I was given hiking socks, a wind up torch, a camping towel, a travel-size first-aid kit, an aluminium thermal mug and a matching one-litre water bottle and dozens of other camping related knick-knacks. My dear son, Michael, with the kindest of hearts and the best of intentions, but more naïve than even I, gave me a rucksack. Not just any old rucksack mind, but a state of the art, top of the range rucksack. What he failed to tell the salesman in the sports shop was that it was for a 1.52 metres, 60 kgs, 70-year-old woman. It was far too big and far too heavy for me, but I didn't fully realise this until much later – too late really because I never lifted it, fully laden, by myself, until my husband left me at Ebbsfleet station where I was to catch the Eurostar train to Paris. Oh yes, I had practised walking with it on my back, but not with it packed to the brim.

I had done a TV interview whilst walking on nearby hills complete with all my hiking gear and empty rucksack, and quite happily walked about for the camera. I did a photo shoot in the park, in all my kit (including the empty rucksack) for a local newspaper and had felt fine. My boots and feet were my greatest concern but, blithe and confident spirit that I am, I was sure that I would have no problems with them or anything else really.

So here I was, totally alone, waiting for the train to Paris, my rucksack beside me where my husband had left it, and with a mini rucksack strapped to my chest with my emergency rations of dried apricots, dark chocolate, shelled almonds, Kendal mint cake and chewing gum - plus a supermarket plastic carrier "bag-for-life" containing drinks and food for the journey and for the first day of my Camino.

Finally, there was my secret "body-bag"!
Strapped around my waist and hidden under my clothes this contained my passport, ready cash and a credit card. Ever the Girl Guide – ever prepared!
The train arrived and I could hardly lift the rucksack that I had so enthusiastically packed, let alone swing it up on to my back. A kindly porter, seeing my plight, helped me on to the train and settled me in to my seat.
I heaved a sigh of relief as I speeded towards Paris. Optimistically, I reassured myself that I would soon "get used to it".

THE BEGINNING

Wednesday 25th March 2009

THE JOURNEY TO PARIS was smooth and uneventful.
I dozed intermittently and between times grew more and
more excited at the prospect of my pilgrimage.
The train arrived at Gare du Nord bang on time and in the
general hustle and bustle eager and helpful people lifted
my rucksack from the train and dumped it on the platform
for me while I strapped my mini-rucksack to my chest and
gathered up my provisions bag.
I had an hour to cross Paris, using the Metro to
Montparnasse – not a lot of time but long enough if I got a
move on. I stood, a little bewildered, trying to get my
bearings as I studied my printed sheet of instructions. The
girl in the travel agent's office had been meticulously
helpful – almost counting out the steps I had to take before
each right or left turn to get me to the correct platform.
Before I even attempted to lift my rucksack a beautiful,
young oriental woman offered to help me. I whispered
thanks to my guardian angel as I lifted one side-strap of
my bag and the smiling oriental woman lifted the other.
'Where to?' she asked,

'Montparnasse,' I replied.

We dodged through the rush hour throng of poker-faced commuters, all marching eyes front, and focused like so many automatons wound up and sent out for the day. The woman obviously knew her way around the Metro and within minutes had me bundled on to a train bound for Montparnasse. I turned to thank her, but she was gone. The train for Irun was already in the station when the Metro pulled in and again eager folk helped me to transfer across, stowed my rucksack and guided me to my seat.

IT ALL SEEMED SO EASY, effortless really; now I was sure that my guardian angels were at work.

The next four hours sped by as I dozed intermittently, or listened to the French grand'-mère sitting opposite me. She took great delight in telling me her entire family history in broken English, the names, gender, ages and marital status of her three children, their occupations and how far up the career ladder each of them had managed to climb, the names, ages and gender of their children, and how talented they all were, and that she was on her way to Bayonne to attend the christening of her latest grandchild. All riveting stuff, but not enough to stop me from getting lost in my own thoughts and my mixed feelings of excitement and apprehension. A huge wave of determination swept over me as I nibbled at some of my picnic provisions; now that I had started, one way or another, I would get all the way to Santiago and collect my Compostela.

At Irun I had a two hour wait for my connecting train to Pamplona, so I left my rucksack with a station guard – I knew that no-one could run off with it! – and went for coffee and a look around the town. The weather was warm and mild and very comforting after the chill winds I had left behind in England.

I strolled along a shopping arcade, glad of the fresh air and exercise after sitting for so many hours. I bought several picture postcards and stamps, and whilst enjoying my second cup of gloriously strong French coffee, I wrote and addressed them to various friends and family members, just to let them know that I was well on my way. I popped the cards in the post box and then with the help of a couple of station porters finally boarded the little local train to Pamplona, where I arrived early that evening - just as dusk was beginning to fall.

I EMERGED FROM THE STATION a little unsteady under my heavy load and not really sure what to do or where to go, so I did a very un-pilgrim thing.

Hailed a taxi!

In halting Spanish, I asked to be taken to the nearest pilgrim refuge.

A multilingual notice pinned to the door explained that the refuge did not open for business until the following month, in readiness for the pilgrim rush of Semana Santa (Holy Week).

What to do next?

I had now been travelling for almost eighteen hours and was quite overcome with exhaustion. I felt and almost certainly must have looked in a frightful state.

A group of students began tumbling, laughing and joking from a nearby language school and it was they who directed me to another refuge on the other side of town. The taxi driver pulled up at what looked to be a private residence but what transpired to be a refuge run by German volunteers - largely for German pilgrims. The taxi driver left and I was ushered into a small, warm and cosy room where three or four other pilgrims were enjoying an easy and relaxed social session before turning in for the night.

As they turned to greet me the look of shock on their faces would have made me laugh under other circumstances, but right then I was too tired to register much at all. The appearance of an old woman with her giant rucksack and other assorted baggage seemed to fill them all with compassion. Their kindness was overwhelming as they welcomed me into their company, made a fresh pot of tea and offered me titbits of snacks from their provisions.

I paid eight euros for my bed for the night and got the first stamp in my pilgrim passport. (Carta de Peregrino). This pilgrim record is used as a proof of pilgrim status and as a record of one's journey. It is usually stamped at one's starting point, and along the Way stamps can be obtained from churches, cathedrals, refuges (otherwise known as refugios, or albergues), town halls (ayuntamientos), some bars and restaurants - and hotels. On arrival at Santiago de Compostela the completed passport can be presented at the Cathedral's Pilgrim Office where a certificate of pilgrimage (compostela) is granted in recognition of achievement in following the Camino.

A volunteer carried my baggage upstairs to a tiny private room, showed me where to find the bathroom and lavatory - and left.

I was far too tired to sleep so I took a sleeping pill and within minutes of crawling into my sleeping-bag I had dropped into oblivion.

MY EYES FLICKERED OPEN – total darkness.
I blinked several times, only blackness.
Panicking, I blinked several times more – nothing!

Fear rising in my throat, I screwed up my eyes as tight as I could then forced them wide open; still inky blackness.
Dear God – had I gone blind?
Overwhelmed by panic and fear I struggled to sit up.
My arms pinioned to my sides, my legs and body trapped in a soft cocoon, in terror my thoughts swirled around in my brain.
The terrifying thought struck me that I'd been buried alive.
Forcing myself to lift my head and shoulders my forehead hit something hard, knocking me backwards. I saw stars and flashing lights. My terror-driven heartbeats sounded like a drum roll in my ears.
Dear God, I screamed inwardly, where am I? What has happened?
I lay still, trying to gather my scattered wits. Tear-drops rolled from the corners of my eyes and ran wet over my cheeks.
Have I been buried alive?' 'Did I hit my head on the coffin lid?
I took a deep breath. Relax! RELAX! Relax! I told myself. More deep breaths; then, Keep calm; keep calm.
Again I blinked, and again – still there was no light at all. One breath – gently in and gently blow out; two breaths in, deeper and deeper then exhale.
Slowly, very slowly, my fear began to subside as my scattered wits assembled and gradually my memory returned.
I was in Pamplona, on the first day of my pilgrimage to Santiago.
Relief swept over me as my mind reluctantly emerged from its deeply drugged slumber.
This was my first experience of sleeping alone, in a sleeping-bag, on the bottom level of a bunk-bed in the

pitch blackness of a heavily shuttered room in a pilgrims' refugio.

PAMPLONA to PUENTE LA REINA

Thursday 26th March 2009 (1st day of walking.)

AFTER THE TRAUMA of my awakening I quickly washed and dressed, re-packed my bag, had a cup of hot water and was soon ready to go.
A fellow pilgrim helped me to get my rucksack on my back and just before 7.00 a.m I made my way through the virtually deserted but incredibly beautiful streets and squares of the cathedral area of the city.
The spaciousness of the parks and gardens and grandeur of the buildings, some of which seemed to shimmer and sparkle in the dazzling early morning sun, was, and is, truly breathtaking.
I had chosen to begin my adventure in Pamplona for several reasons, one of them being that I am a great fan of the works of Ernest Hemingway and had long wanted to see the city that was so beloved by him and about which he wrote so enticingly.

A second reason was my own fascination with all things related to the Roman Empire.

Pamplona has been the capital of the Navarre region of Spain since the 9th Century. Legend has it that it has been a fortress town since the days of the Roman Empire and was possibly founded by Pompey the Great and named after him as Pompaelo.

The third and most important reason was because last year I had, due to severe arthritis, the big toe joint (bunion) on my left foot replaced with a rigid metal rod. I had spent three months with a plaster almost up to my knee and been forced to keep that foot in a non-weight-bearing position for all of that time.

To facilitate this the hospital had issued me with a contraption that looked like a child's scooter – with adaptations. They taught me how to manoeuvre myself around by kneeling on my left leg and propelling the thing by my right leg.

Easier to do when you are seven than when you are seventy!

But now - ? Freedom!

EVEN WITH TWO WALKING STICKS I didn't feel confident enough with my replacement joint to begin my pilgrimage in Saint-Jean-Pied-de-Post in France, the usual starting place when walking the Camino, and face the snow-covered Pyrenees – so Pamplona it was!

I passed a café in a quiet square with tables already set outside. The smell of fresh coffee was so enticing, and as there were no other customers about I decided I would practise getting my rucksack off and then on again – unaided.

I ordered milky coffee and a croissant with butter and jam and whilst the waiter was busy I turned my back to a table, bent my knees until my burden was resting on the table top and then undid the straps – bingo! No problem: and I was also able to get it back on again the same way, only in reverse order.

Rucksack thus sorted – as long as there was always a convenient table or table substitute available, I would be OK.

I was sorry not to be able to spend more time in Pamplona, but after a quick "loo" stop and without further dalliance I was once more on my way.

Once I had left the city and its suburbs behind, the scenery was spectacular, but I was too overwhelmed by the unseasonable heat and very effort of walking under the weight of my heavy load to fully enjoy the beauty of it all. The bird song and wild flowers were exquisite and I managed to capture some of it on my video camera. Apart from two cyclists who whizzed by me with a bright 'buenos dias', I didn't see another soul. On a positive note there was no-one to see me climb or descend the Alto de Perdon sideways, crab-fashion with the aid of my two sticks – or every time I found a stone wall or tree stump that would substitute as a table-top, see me take an opportunistic "loo" stop.

When I finally arrived at Puente la Reina it had taken me eight hours to travel 24 kilometres (15 miles.) The sight of the pilgrim statue and the Albergue Jakue close by released floods of tears – some of relief, others for the sheer joy of having managed to complete my first day's walking in one piece.

Utterly exhausted and drenched in sweat I literally staggered into the pilgrim dormitory. My feet were fine, my boots were doing a splendid job, but the ache in my thighs and buttocks was excruciating. Shedding my load was utter bliss and the cool of the albergue so welcome after the sweltering heat of the day.

When my eyes became accustomed to the half light I noticed a woman resting on a top bunk. I nodded and waved 'Hello.'

'Your bag is too big and looks to be too heavy', was all she said.

My thoughts ran along the retort of 'Smart arse, stating the bleeding obvious,' but with a demure smile, I refrained, and said: 'I know. I have just carried it for over eight hours'. She didn't speak to me again!

I was desperately tired, my shoulders and the small of my back ached every bit as much as my buttocks and thighs and I was ravenously hungry, having only nibbled on my emergency rations of dried apricots, chocolate raisins, almonds and Kendal mint cake all day.

I went upstairs to the café and saw a man sitting there in the sun with his bare feet propped up on a table. He beckoned me over and as I approached I could see blisters almost the size of my fist on the ball of each of his feet. He lifted a balloon-sized glass of red wine in acknowledgement – 'Salute'. We shook hands and he told me his name was Pieter, from Poland. I sat beside him and asked the waiter to bring me the menu and a bottle of water. I swear that nectar could not have tasted better than that ice cool aqua minerale – con gas!

I enjoyed my first proper meal in two days – a perfectly cooked tuna fish steak and a crunchy fresh salad washed down with a glass of Rioja, courtesy of Pieter, who had now obligingly removed his feet from the table and placed them delicately on a chair. With the back of his hand, he brushed away the tears that began streaming down his face as he told me that he had come all the way from

Warsaw but this was the end of his Camino – his feet having let him down.

Ten minutes later, still barefoot, he hobbled off on his heels into a taxi heading back to Pamplona.

The percentage of pilgrims who drop out along the Way is very high. Again I renewed my vow that I would not be one of them. Come what may, I would reach Santiago. After my meal I took a gentle stroll along the main street, meandered along a side-turning and prepared to make my way back to the albergue - when I found an old church. The door was open so I decided to take a few minutes of quiet meditation. The inside was cool and it took a couple of seconds for my eyes to adjust to the darkness. As I looked around I marvelled at the beautiful simplicity of it all, then my eyes were attracted to what looked like a life-size silver swan. It was the baptismal font, exquisite in every tiny detail and so amazing, almost incredible really, to find such a treasure tucked away and unprotected in a tiny local church.

I was showered and in bed by eight-o'clock.

No need for a sleeping pill tonight - I was out for the count in minutes.

PUENTE LA REINA to CIRAUQUI

Friday 27th March 2009 (2nd day of walking.)

YESTERDAY MORNING I HAD AWOKEN thinking at worst that I had been buried alive, at best that I had gone blind in the night.
Today I was sure I was paralysed.
I couldn't move a muscle in my arms or my legs.
From my neck down, my entire body was just one dull, heavy ache.
I lay still in the half light, afraid to move, cursing myself for being so stubborn yesterday, for walking so far, for being so stupid, so damned determined!
I heard people moving about and managed to look at the clock on the wall.
It was 5.40 a.m.
What on earth is happening? Is there a fire or something? Are they all mad?
I moved my shoulders gently, gingerly up to my ears then down again. I repeated this simple movement twice more.

I heaved a heavy sigh of relief. Well, at least some of my muscles worked.

The woman from the bunk above mine, the smart ass from yesterday, told me in no uncertain terms that I should get up and get going before the heat of the day made walking uncomfortable. What a bossy, boring cow she is, I thought, but said nothing.

I flexed my right elbow and managed to pull open the zip of my sleeping-bag.

Would my legs move now?

Slowly I swung them round and tenderly placed my feet on the cold, tiled floor, then very carefully unfolded the rest of myself from the bed. Unbearable pain in my buttocks and behind my thighs seared down to my ankles. Bent almost double, I shuffled and slid off to the bathroom. Each movement was an untold agony. I was surely paying a penance for my perseverance of yesterday. Shuffle, shuffle - back to bed and back to sleep.

I woke again to the sound of the cleaner sweeping and mopping the floors. It was 8.00 a.m. The notice above the kitchen work bench warned all pilgrims to be gone by 8.00 a.m. Dredging strength from my deepest psyche my reluctant body doggedly re-assembled itself. Slowly I managed to drag on my clothes and roll up my sleeping-bag and nightclothes as each movement sent a searing agony through my shoulders, legs and arms.

I decided to lighten my load at least a little, so left behind a plastic plate, a knife, fork and spoon – future pilgrims for the use of!

With grim determination I staggered upstairs to the café for coffee, hot croissants, butter and jam - surely the morning food of the gods!

Three coffees later, warmed and slightly more relaxed by the morning sun, I slowly and painstakingly hoisted my bag on to my back and set off again on to the pilgrim trail. After only a few hundred metres I reached the eleventh century pilgrim bridge, from which the town derived its name. The river Arga sparkled and rippled on its way. The six arches of the bridge, virtually unchanged from the time they were built, were reflected in all of their ancient beauty in the twinkling waters. Glad of an excuse to stop and rest I wriggled my rucksack onto the balustrade and carefully freed my arms and shoulders. Resting my bag at my feet I couldn't resist taking photographs of the river and the tranquil area beside it, and wonder at the thousands of pilgrim feet that had trod this way before me.

I managed to travel five kilometres more, then in a state of near collapse I shambled into the first bar I came to in Maneru, to answer the call of nature, to rest my aching body and to replenish my need for caffeine.

Again I had not met another soul on the way.

Three kilometres later and I reached Cirauqui.

Enough was enough for one day – my body could take no more. I wept silent tears as the excruciating pain in my legs and shoulders knifed through to my very bones.

The village was quiet, the tiny square deserted and the sun beat down remorselessly.

The refugio was closed until 3.00 p.m. so I sat in the sun, on the steps of the church to let the heat relax and heal my aching muscles. I read my pilgrim guide and snacked on some of my emergency rations, my almonds, dried apricots and cranberries coated in thick, dark chocolate washed down with lots of water.

After a while I managed a few simple yoga exercises which helped to loosen some of the knotted muscles across my shoulders, but my arms, legs and buttocks refused to let go of the clenching agony that held them in a relentless grasp. The church clock struck two, and seemingly coming from nowhere swarms of workmen emerged, heading towards the bar. Tempting smells of cooking food wafted in the air, so just like a Bisto Kid I followed the workmen. As I opened the bar door the loud buzz, drone and babble of the men's rapid repartee interspersed with loud bursts of laughter jarred painfully on my ear drums. After the bright sunshine it took a few moments for my eyes to adjust to the gloom. A thick blue fug of tobacco smoke hung in the air and stung my eyes. A long trestle table was placed in the centre, from one end of the room to the other. The men were seated on rough wooden benches in long rows on either side of it. They were silent for a second or two when they noticed me enter the bar, but then quickly resumed their banter and chatter.

A waitress dealt out menus like a blackjack dealer in Vegas, then dished out bottles of water and wine while at the same time scribbling orders on her little note pad. I hesitated, then gingerly approached the table. One of the men turned to me and half-rose to his feet in acknowledgement.

'May I join you?' I asked in my halting Spanish.

The men shuffled along, making room for me to sit on the end of the bench. The waitress handed me a menu. I noticed conejo (rabbit) was on there and salivated at the thought of a lovely stew with tasty juices, so nodded, pointed to my choice, and settled back in anticipation. The plates were served by the same blackjack dealer and mine held rabbit alright, but it was skinned, roasted and halved from nose to tail along its spine, lying stretched flat out on the plate with one baleful eye staring up at me. I choked, swallowed hard, then cupped a hand over my mouth, completely unable to face eating it. I pushed the plate away. The man next to me turned a quizzical gaze in my direction, furrowed his brow and shrugged his shoulders.

'No me gusta – I don't like it', I whispered, whereupon he scraped the carcass across onto his own plate and tucked into it with obvious delight.

Back in the bright sunshine I made my way towards the albergue. Crowds of young pilgrims jostled and joked together in the square. Although, seemingly all from different countries they all used English with ease and aplomb. As I approached they stopped their playful, boisterous antics and stood in silence, watching me. I felt like a hearse at a funeral. Slowly they clustered around me, seemingly incredulous that I was even there, and began to bombard me with questions, such as:

Where was I from?

How far had I walked?

Did I realise that my bag was too big?

I dropped my rucksack on the ground beside me and one tall, athletic young man lifted it up. He let out a stream of expletives in I don't know what language, and suddenly all the young men were competing to see who could most readily lift my bag, all of them obviously impressed that I had carried it so far. They each had miniature bags that I swear could hold no more than a pair of spare socks and knickers!

The doors of the albergue swung open and with a wave of her arm and a beaming smile a homely Spanish woman beckoned us inside.

The youngsters all jostled for beds and by the time I had carried myself and my bag up the steps and booked in, most of the beds had already been "bagged". I found a space in a tiny room, no more than twelve feet by ten.

Three bunk-beds were placed in a U shape around the walls, leaving hardly any space for movement or manoeuvre.

Although most of the beds were taken up by young pilgrims, one was occupied by a massive, six-feet-six-inches tall, grizzled old German man who weighed probably in excess of 230 pounds. From the smell of him he hadn't showered for days or even weeks, and the only ventilation in the room was one small window set high in the wall opposite the door.

We shared a delicious communal meal which had been prepared by the woman who ran the albergue (hostelera.) After my earlier experience I chose the vegetarian option of bean stew and fresh crusty bread with a glass of rough, local wine. It was such a feast and such warm and hearty company. I said little but listened and marvelled at the exuberance and energy of the young people.

Later, after a cold shower, (I discovered that the trick is to get showered as soon as you can after arriving at a refugio as there is almost always a limited amount of hot water) I sat quietly with the Spanish woman as she knitted an intricate, multi-coloured bed spread.

I had given her my box of baby wet-wipes and my yoga mat.

We talked, she in halting English and I in broken Spanish, of our lives, loves, hopes and dreams.

We were joined by a surly, six-foot tall, young Dutch girl. She seemed to be fuelled with anger and from her attitude obviously had issues with older women (or maybe just her mother!) She was blonde, blue-eyed and angular, with a face like a thoroughbred racehorse. In perfect English that rasped with aggression and with machine gun rapidity, she began firing at me:

'Why are you here?

'You are too old! The Camino is too difficult and dangerous for old women.

'You should be at home with your family.'

I didn't answer. I looked her straight in the eye, nodding agreement all the while as she ranted on and on. Finally, she huffed a great sigh and flounced off to the showers. I hoped that they were still cold!

I was in bed by 8.00 p.m.

With six of us in a room no bigger than my bathroom at home, I was grateful that the window was wide open to give at least a breath of fresh air.

Nevertheless I soon dropped into a deep and contented sleep.

CIRAUQUI to VIANNA

Saturday 28th March 2009 (3rd day of walking.)

THE NEXT THING I KNEW the place was a hive of activity and bustle.
People were stripping beds, rolling up sleeping-bags and packing rucksacks.
There was nothing for it: although it was only 5.00 a.m. I joined in the scuffle and packing and was on the road soon after six.
Although still nagging away my aches and pains were not as severe as they had been, and I was able to enjoy the glory of the sky at sunrise and the beautiful countryside. Most of the pilgrims strode off at a hearty pace, but even with my bag at least a kilo lighter without my yoga mat and box of baby wipes, I was soon left well behind.
I was happy to have time alone for quiet contemplation and was almost moved to tears as the dawn chorus swelled from the throats of a multitude of birds, filling the sky all around me with heavenly sounds.

Apart from struggling up a fairly steep climb to the village of Lorca, the path was largely downhill: I covered the ten kilometres to Estella almost totally alone and without hitch or problem.

I headed straight for the town centre where I soon found a café where I could rest awhile and enjoy my usual morning treat of milky coffee, warm croissants, jam and butter.

A couple of "older" women, complete with rucksacks and scallop shells walked past the window. The scallop shell is the symbol of the Camino de Santiago. As a guide to pilgrims they are seen frequently on posts or walls along The Way. They are seen even more commonly on pilgrims themselves, because the wearing of a shell denotes that one is a traveller on the Camino. The shell is also linked metaphorically, and by myths and legends, as an emblem of St. James.

In answer to my silent prayer, the two women turned around and came into the café. Thank you - angels!

Soon a third woman joined them.

As they discarded their rucksacks I caught the eye of one of them and beckoned them to join me. They introduced themselves as Carol from the USA, Hannah from Switzerland, who having worked for ten years as an au pair in London spoke perfect English, and finally . . . the aptly named Gaby – a garrulous Australian.

They were an exuberant group, very warm and welcoming.

Gaby had been bitten half to death the night before by bed bugs. She had been to the pharmacy for something to soothe her itches. She said that she couldn't get out of Estella fast enough, so they were all taking a bus to Vianna. They invited me to join them.

Oh how quickly I yielded to temptation!

The joy of being with a bunch of relaxed, easy going women was wonderful.

The bus took 40 minutes and cost just 3.29 euros – bargain! It was exactly what I needed but it wasn't long before my conscience began pricking me as I watched the countryside whizz by. Was this cheating - I wondered? If it was then, who was I cheating? I argued with myself. Who makes the rules?

I eased my pangs of guilt by deciding that even medieval pilgrims would not have been averse to hitching a ride on a passing hay cart. Anyway, my guide book says that to gain a compostela a pilgrim must cover the last 100 kilometres to Santiago by foot or the last 200 kilometres on horseback - or by bicycle.

Apparently though, some people who miss part of the Camino often feel compelled to return at some future time to re-do their pilgrimage.

I once met a woman at a gathering of the Confraternity in London who told me that the year before she had had to take her injured walking companion to hospital by bus and train and that the detour had taken out over 60 miles from her trek. She told me she was planning to repeat her pilgrimage, but this time in full!

(In fact she did this and whilst walking met the love of her life, her soul mate. Who says that the Camino doesn't have magical forces?)

My three new friends and I booked into the Albergue Andreas Munoz in Vianna as soon as it opened at noon. It was fabulously clean and new.

We left our bags and went off together to explore the town.

One of my greatest pleasures at home is sharing time with my many female friends – here was a substitute. After two days of being virtually alone in the world I so needed this camaraderie, friendship and light easy banter. My spirits fizzed and bubbled with delight.

We soon found a bar with an impressive array of local foods and an abundant range of wines, beers and speciality ciders. Spoiled for choice we ordered foaming tankards of beer and an assortment of dishes to share.
 Lovely!

I decided that meeting these women was my first Camino miracle!

When we finally emerged into the bright afternoon sunshine all the shops were shut, but we found a bakery where we bought fresh bread and eggs and a few other goodies – enough for dinner, breakfast and a packed meal for tomorrow.

In the street we bumped into Dan, a friend of Carol's, so we joined him for a beer and a chat to share our Camino experiences so far.

Back in the albergue, Gaby taught me how to use my tiny video camera and we spent a hilarious time practising by filming all and sundry in all manner of comic poses and pulling of silly faces. I felt incredibly happy and relaxed, with no thought of being so far from home.

We shared the cost of the provisions and chores in the albergue.

Carol and Hannah cooked dinner – a delicious lentil soup, scrambled egg and orange segments for dessert. Gaby and I washed up and cleaned the kitchen before we all went to the church of Santa Maria for a short mass, and also to get our pilgrim passports stamped.

After he had been speared to death here in 1507, the grave of Cesare Borgia is said to be either inside, or outside of the church door - depending on who tells the story. The

priest assured us that it was outside the church and
showed us the commemorative stone to prove it.

Back at the albergue our small (six-bed) dormitory was full
of women. Nicoletta was from Italy, with legs, I swear,
that were at least a metre long! She wore black silk
stockings and a black suspender belt under her hiking
trousers. Surely only an Italian would aspire to such chic!
The rest of us, Heidi from Germany, Hannah, Gaby, Carol
and I stripped off our more mundane gear with giggles
and chit-chat. The atmosphere soon disintegrated into an
episode that could have been pure St. Trinian's.

It took me ages to get to sleep as my mind replayed the
glorious events of the day.

I had never anticipated being so happy on my pilgrimage
or sharing such marvellous, friendly, female company. I
decided to leave behind a handtowel and a box of hot
chocolate mix – other pilgrims for the use of!

VIANNA to NAVARRETE

Sunday 29th March 2009 (4th day of walking.)

I AWOKE TO A GLORIOUS MORNING, one of sunshine and sweet air, reminiscent of early summer in England. My aches and pains were still nagging across my shoulders, but bearable. I was quite amazed at the way my feet and legs were keeping in such trouble-free good shape, but still left nothing to chance and massaged them with soothing foot cream before putting on my socks and boots.

I shared a relaxed communal breakfast, the room full of friendly pilgrim banter, and then packed my rucksack and prepared for a good day's walking.

We set off before eight at a fairly leisurely pace. I walked for a while with Carol who told me she was 71-years-old and had initially trained as a nurse, but had then chosen to become a nun, in holy orders, where she remained for many years until she'd met Henry, a priest. They had fallen madly and deeply in love, and after much soul-searching and heartache had each decided to leave behind their holy orders and marry. Because she was already a trained nurse she had soon found work in a large hospital, while Henry trained in social work. They had five children, now all grown and living their own independent lives.

Carol and Henry had led a contented, happy life together for thirty-five years. She told me that Dan, who we had met yesterday, was a long time friend of her family and that he had also been a priest who had fallen in love with a woman and quit holy orders to marry. Apparently this was his sixth Camino. It was because of him relating his past Camino experiences that Carol had decided to travel with him to Spain to make her own pilgrimage. She had met Gaby and Hannah, by chance, at St. Jean-Pied-de Port, struck up an instant friendship with them both and they had travelled together this far.

Later I walked with Hannah. She told me of her years as an au pair in London, and how after more than forty years she still keeps in touch with the family. She told me that her husband, Guiseppe, was making the pilgrimage with her, but had decided to walk yesterday rather than take the bus. He was with a Dutchman, Joseph, and they all planned to meet in Logrono for tapas.

Hannah told me that she and her husband worked a small farm in Switzerland. They had a son who helped them run the place, but she was worried about him as he was now thirty-eight and still unmarried. She told me that she and Guiseppe were offering up their pilgrimage in the hope that their son would find a wife. I thought he might stand a better chance finding one if he did the camino himself, but said nothing!

The walk was relaxed and fairly uneventful, except for my rucksack, which even after discarding a couple of kilos was still too heavy — but it was manageable.

High in the hills, a few kilometres before Logrono, we came upon a tiny cottage. It looked a perfect home for Hansel and Gretel, but in fact - according to my guide book - it belonged to Doña Felisa. As we approached, a Spanish woman who looked as old as the hills around her and was dressed from head to toe in black, waved her arm in welcome, and called out a friendly 'Buenos dias'.

She stood in wait for us beside a small kitchen table and old folding chair, which transpired to be her "stamping station"! One after the other we offered her our pilgrim passports which she ceremoniously branded with her own particular crest. This consisted of a fig and its leaf, a jug of water, two more figs and a cross, and the motto: higos-aqua y amor (figs-water and love). She held out her hand for donations and we all duly crossed her palm with coins. The saying goes that anyone who does not get a stamp here has not done a proper pilgrimage.

The old woman's daughter came out of the house to join us and beckoned us in to try her fresh orange juice, for a few cents a glass.

'Tiene servicios?' I asked ('Do you have a toilet'?)

'No tiene,' the old woman replied; 'lo siento, pero sola pee-pee detras de la casa'.

We all collapsed into a fit of the giggles when we realised she was telling us that she had no toilet for public use, but we were quite at liberty to take a pee – and nothing else!- at the back of her cottage.

We arrived at Logrono at noon where we found Joseph and Guiseppe sitting outside a bar in the square in front of the church of Santiago el Real.

Hannah's husband, Guiseppe, was an adorable little man. I swear he could have been the model for countless garden gnomes, complete with beard and a little hat. It is surprising how quickly friendships are made and forged on the Camino. I took to Guiseppe instantly and almost loved him like an old friend. I marvelled at the tender way he greeted Hannah, hugged her and eased off her rucksack.

Joseph, Guiseppe's Dutch friend, was big - well over six-feet tall - and burly, but not fat. Probably aged about sixty, he immediately presented as being a kind and gentle man, who made me feel perfectly at ease.

He helped me take off my rucksack, and organised chairs for everyone. We all shared tapas and beer and gentle, convivial conversation, catching up on the Way so far. They decided they would walk on to Navarette – another 12 kilometres, making 26 kilometres for the day. I was really apprehensive, not knowing whether the pace would be quicker when the men were walking with us and thinking it was quite a punishing trek anyway, wondering if it would be too much for me with my still heavy load. On the other hand I was so enjoying their company that I didn't want to lose them.

I set off with the group, but after a while I lagged behind a little and walked alone, pondering. I felt confused, inept and totally inadequate. Almost everyone I had met so far had seemed to have a purpose:

Why was I doing this? My efforts felt like an empty gesture - to what?

What was the Camino all about anyway?

After a while Joseph dropped back from the group and walked beside me. We fell into quiet conversation. I told him that my husband was a Dutchman from "den Bosch" and that I had stayed in various parts of Holland during the 1960s and '70s.

He told me that he was a scout leader, hence the Baden-Powell type hat he was wearing. He said this was his third pilgrimage. We moved on to talk of our faiths, our beliefs about God and the universe, and life in general. It transpired that he was a deeply religious catholic with strongly held, but not dogmatic, views of right and wrong. He told me his wife had an aggressive form of breast cancer and that he was offering this pilgrimage up for her. I was deeply moved and lost for words, when Gaby joined us.

The conversation turned to travel. Gaby told us that she had taken a sabbatical year to visit places of interest to her, and was travelling all around the world. Walking the Camino was an important part of her itinerary. She talked of her failed marriage and her struggle to raise her son alone. He is now 21-years-old and doing fine, working as a car mechanic. She showed us pictures of her new partner, Sam, who at twenty-nine is twenty years her junior. He looked a gorgeous hunk of Australian manhood and I wondered why she had taken a year out and left him behind. I couldn't help wondering how long a young, healthy, red-blooded male would stay faithful and celibate. But, hey, what do I know? So I said nothing!

It was late afternoon when I finally reached Navarrete. I was utterly exhausted. My pace had slowed down somewhat and the others had all walked ahead of me. I was quite content to carry on in my own time, but dear sweet Guiseppe had left his bag at the albergue and walked back nearly a mile to help me carry mine.

The one pilgrim "bedroom" room was fairly small, about 15ft x 15ft with five bunk-beds strategically arranged to maximise the available space. By the time I checked in and got to the room there were no bottom bunks free, and not having the energy to climb the ladder to a top one I almost wept with despair and tiredness.

Sensing my distress, Joseph immediately volunteered to offer up his bottom bunk for me. I was overwhelmed by his sensitivity and kindness and too near to tears to offer more than a whispered and heartfelt, 'Thank you'. Within seconds I dropped, fully clothed, on to the proffered bunk and slept like a baby for an hour.

When I awoke the others had all showered, changed and done some clothes-washing, all of which was drying nicely on the line outside. I quickly showered - luckily the water was still warm - changed into some clean clothes and stuffed my dirty gear into the washing machine, then we all walked together into the village for a meal. It was a warm and balmy evening so we decided to sit outside to enjoy the good local food and wines.

Life at this stage of the Camino was very convivial. I am not sure what I had expected but it certainly wasn't anything as pleasant as this.

Back at the albergue I parcelled up all my cosmetics and most of my toiletries ready to post back to England in the morning – another kilo less in my rucksack!

Pamploma at daybreak

My collection of shells

Pilgrim statue in Puenta la Reina

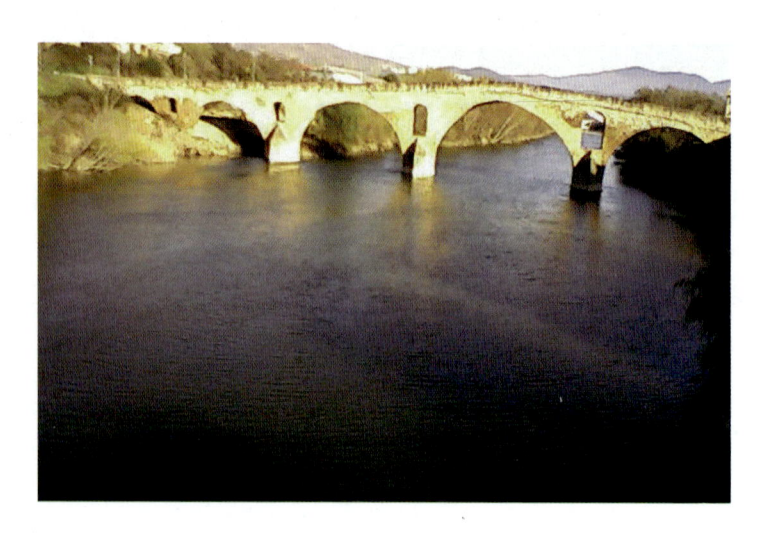

The ancient bridge in Puenta la Reina

Albergue at Cirauqui

A marker along the way

My young Spanish companions: Lara, Olga and Miguel

Leper statue in Burgos

A blissful foot massage

In the albergue at Fromista

With Miguel near Carrion de los Condes

Lunch in the sunshine at Leon

Outside the cathedral in Leon

The rosary made by the old man at Foncebadon

Cruz de Ferro (Iron Cross) on Monte Irago

NAVARRETE to NAJERE

Monday 30th March 2009 (5th day of walking)

THE WEATHER CONTINUED TO BE VERY PLEASANT, warm and sunny with only the lightest of breezes. Joseph, Guiseppe, Carol, Gaby and Hannah headed off towards Najere, and I spent an hour exploring the medieval streets of Navarrete while waiting for the post office to open.

My bag was minus quite a few things by now, but it didn't feel any lighter. However, I was getting used to carrying it. Luckily my feet were fine, with no sign of blisters or callouses. My buttocks and the backs of my thighs still ached remorselessly whenever I was walking uphill or descending from a peak, but I could live with that.

It was strange to be walking alone again after being in a convivial group for two days. After about an hour of it, with a rush of blood to the head I suddenly realised that I had stupidly left my clothes in the washing machine back at the albergue.

Blast!

There was no going back for them though, even if it meant losing my best red bra and favourite black leggings.

Leaving Navarrete the Camino's route became a gentle climb over hills dotted with vineyards, all the way up towards Ventosa where I met up with Carol, Gaby and Hannah again – the men having wanted a brisker walk had headed off to Azofra.

The next few kilometres, after the Alto de San Anton, were mostly a gentle descent that reminded me of walking parts of the South Downs Way in Sussex.

Our little group seemed more subdued today, and unenthusiastic – or maybe it was just me. We finally brightened up a little as we approached Najera, only to be confronted by a huge bill-board (at least three metres long) with wording in German, which Hannah explained was a poem written by an anonymous poet and described his (or her) feelings during the pilgrimage. It said:-

Why do I accept the dry dust in my mouth
The mud on my aching feet
The lashing rain and the glaring sun on my skin?
Because of the beautiful towns?
Because of the churches?
Because of the food?
Because of the wine?
No! Because I was summoned!

Is that why we are all here?
It suddenly seemed to me to be quite ridiculous to be walking, walking, walking across the top of Spain to some place connected to some mythical person lost in the ages old mists of time.
Was I summoned?

Is that the answer?

Surely not!

It was at this point in my musings that the tongue of my left boot suddenly developed a mind of its own and began twisting and rubbing against my ankle. I took off the boot and re-laced it, but after only a few minutes walking the tongue was twisted again. I stopped and dug in my rucksack for an extra sock, put it on and re-laced my boot once more. By the time I got to the albergue I had a nasty sore and painful area right across my left instep. That will teach me to question the whys and wherefores of the Camino.

The albergue was bright and sunny with a large communal dining/social area. There was a small supermarket next door where we bought provisions and cooked ourselves another shared meal.

A self-invited Frenchman joined our table and became very chatty and, annoyingly, over-friendly towards me. He asked if he could walk with me the next day. I told him that I did not want to walk with him, in fact I didn't want to get involved with him at all. He was ultra oily and persistent and hung around our little group for hours, seemingly oblivious to all the cold-shoulder and ignoring behaviour we presented to him. He seemed to be in his mid-to-late-50s and I wondered what kind of a pervert he was. Why was he chasing after older women when there was a wide selection of females of every age, size and shape in the albergue?

NAJERE to VILORIA DE RIOJA

Tuesday 31st March 2009 (6th day of walking)

THE NEXT MORNING the Frenchman was as amorous as ever towards me. I was more than a little afraid of him so I decided to take a bus for a few kilometres in order to shake him off.
We left early and the girls walked on while I took a bus from the terminal – but to my absolute horror the Frenchman followed me! I was beginning to feel really scared of him, so I bought a ticket to Santo Domingo de la Calzada, 20 kilometres away, sure that he wouldn't go that far and I would finally be rid of him – but no such luck. He sat beside me all the way and didn't seem in the least perturbed or put out when I refused to speak to him or to answer any of his questions. Then I almost wept when I realised that in my anxiety to be off and away from the Frenchman I had again forgotten to collect my washing

from the tumble drier – this time I had lost two pairs of socks, one pair of leggings and a T shirt top.

When I got off the bus I dashed to the nearest café. My heart leaped with joy and relief when I saw Dan, Carol's friend that I had met in Vianna, enjoying a leisurely breakfast and quiet read of a guide book. I asked if he would mind if I joined him, and he patted the chair beside him and helped me off with my ruck-sack.

To my absolute chagrin the Frenchman had the gall to follow me into the café as well. Now I was really afraid and very angry over this transparently blatant and persistent pursuit of me. I whispered my predicament urgently to Dan and asked if he could help me. I could feel the Frenchman's eyes burning in to me from where he stood up at the bar. I pretended to be engrossed in Dan's guide book while he ordered coffee and croissants for me. Whilst I ate Dan told me the ages old legend of the cock and hen.

Apparently, 700 or so years ago, a family of three pilgrims stayed at an inn in the town. The daughter of the innkeeper took a fancy to the teenage son, Hugonell, and when her advances were rejected by him she put some silver in to the boy's luggage, then denounced him as a thief to the authorities. In those days the punishment for theft was death and the unfortunate young man was hanged.

The distraught parents completed their pilgrimage, and on their return journey found their son still hanging - but alive - with his feet being supported by St. James. The boy's parents appealed to the bishop of Santo Domingo to pardon their son, but the bishop (in the middle of enjoying a hearty chicken dinner) denied their appeal. He is alleged to have said: 'Your son is as guilty as this chicken is dead.' Whereupon the bird flapped its wings and flew up from the plate. The boy was proved innocent, and ever since then a rooster and a hen have been kept in a gilded cage in the cathedral. A right "cock and hen" story, I thought. If you believe that you'll believe anything! However, I have heard several variations on that theme since so I suppose there must be some tiny element of truth hidden somewhere in the annals of time.

Eventually the Frenchman went to the lavatory. I took my chance, and with Dan's help quickly buckled on my rucksack.

'Please try to delay him for me Dan,' I beseeched him as I made a hasty exit from the café. My innards were churning and my breathing laboured as I hastened to make my escape.

The path was a gentle climb with a busy main road on my right hand side, and rolling hills and valleys as far as the eye could see on the other. Fuelled by fear my legs seemed to take on a life of their own and I managed a good steady pace, soon leaving the town far behind. However, no matter how I tried I couldn't calm my bowels. With my anxiety levels off the radar, terrified of stopping in case the Frenchman was following me, I swung from griping stomach cramps to cold rivers of sweat running down my spine – this even though the sun was now hot and high in the sky.

Overcome by fear, nauseous bile rose in my throat and I desperately struggled to be free of my rucksack. At the same time a volcanic eruption seemed to explode in the pit of my stomach. In seconds my rucksack and jacket were off and my trousers down round my ankles, crumpled round my thick socks and boots as the physical manifestation of my fear and anxiety simultaneously exploded from both ends of my body.

The crisis passed, sipping warm water from my bottle and wiping my face with a damp tissue, I offered up a silent prayer of thanks that I had managed to strip in time and avert a seriously messy and disastrous clothing calamity. After once more setting myself to rights, with the help of a nearby tree stump I managed to hoist my rucksack onto my back. With just enough strength left in my legs to begin walking at a snail's pace I set off for Granon, hoping to cover the six kilometres in about an hour-and-a-half to arrive there in time for lunch.

Two hours later, I don't know how I had managed it, but it was obvious that I was hopelessly lost. No matter how hard and carefully I looked there was no sign of any scallop shell way markings, no yellow arrows, and no buildings. No matter which way I turned there was nothing on the horizon that I could use as a guide. I had been so deep in my thoughts I couldn't remember how long it had been since I had seen a way marker, or indeed when I had left the path that ran parallel to the main road. I strained my ears but could not hear the noise of traffic. I was still climbing steadily. That reassured me – sooner or later I would reach a summit and maybe the view of a village, farm or some other landmark that would guide me back on track.

After another fifteen minutes walking I stopped to take a drink and noticed a solitary figure some 500 metres or so behind me. My blood froze and my throat shrunk tight in terror – whoever it was there was no way I could escape and the figure was rapidly gaining on me. I was as transfixed as a rabbit caught in headlights.

Please God don't let it be the Frenchman.

Alleluia! – another Camino miracle . . .

. . . it was Dan.

My heart leaped with joy - Thank you angels!

'I am so pleased to see you.' I gasped as a shuddering sigh of relief shook its way through my body. Fighting back tears I smiled and whispered to my friend – 'I am but totally lost.'

Dan raised one eyebrow and smiled at me, with his map and compass in his hand: 'How funny you should say that,' he said . . . 'so am I!'

Hmm, Yes, I thought. Your sixth Camino, with your map and compass to help you – and you say you're lost? - but I said nothing.

We walked on in companionable silence together for almost half-an-hour, and reached the crest of a hill. A farmhouse nestled in the valley below. Soon we reached a crossroads of several tracks, one of which obviously led down to the farmhouse. Still there were no sign of any way marks. The dilemma was – do we carry on the path we have travelled so far, or turn on to the farm track and head in the direction away from the farm?

Dan decided we should carry straight on.

He walked much more quickly than me, but I gritted my teeth, upped the ante, and managed to keep him in sight as he headed off into the distance.

Within half-an-hour I saw what looked like a church and a group of buildings clustered beside a made up road. Had I found Granon?

I entered an old stone building that seemed to be neither church nor monastery, but transpired to be a hermitage that was also a refugio, café and bar that was obviously also a meeting place for the local community, as the customers seemed to know and greet each other on first name terms.

Dan was already seated at a small table with a beer in front of him, studying the menu. For the second time that day I asked if I could join him and again he helped me to take off my rucksack. A vibrantly cheerful señora took our order and then invited us to see the ancient church at the back of the hermitage.

The church had much of its 16th century glass and stonework still intact. It was a beautiful and tranquil space for quiet meditation - even though it was coated in a fine layer of dust and draped in cobwebs.

I asked Dan what had happened to the Frenchman, and he told me he had related our cock and hen tale to him, and had then persuaded him to visit the Cathedral with him. He had niftily slipped away, leaving the Frenchman deep in conversation with a priest there. (Thankfully I never saw the Frenchman again, but I made a vow that one day I will return to Santo Domingo de la Calzada to see the Cathedral for myself.)

Whilst we ate our meal Dan told me some of his story and how and why he had left the priesthood. He said he had been very happy with his wife and their joy was unbounded when they had a baby daughter. Sadly, when the daughter was only ten-years-old his wife had died. The girl was traumatised by the death of her mother and presented Dan with untold variants of difficult behaviours. He explained that she was now in her late twenties and still caused him heartache and problems. He confessed that he had done many Caminos, as penance for leaving the priesthood and to plead for emotional strength and help to deal with his daughter and her ongoing psychological difficulties.

Dan left ahead of me, but before I could reflect on his story the woman who had shown us around the church sat beside me and offered to walk with me to the edge of the village, to ensure that I was on the right trail. She told me that some unscrupulous villagers often turned the sign posts around and directed unsuspecting pilgrims away from the trail and into the gardens of restaurants and bars in order to gain more local custom!

We said our goodbyes and I thanked the lady for her help and kindness.

Seeing Dan in the valley in the far distance, I set off to follow him.

Lost in my thoughts again I could only marvel at the size of the wide open spaces and the incredible differences in each region. Leaving behind the vineyards and fertile greenery of La Rioja I was now nearing the region of Burgos, and before me stretched sweeping swathes of wheat fields. Dan was now only a tiny black speck on the horizon and I suddenly felt totally alone in the world.

A minute later I dissolved into and was blinded by floods of tears.

Thinking of Dan's story about his daughter I realised that it was exactly sixty years to the day that my mother had died – when I was also ten-years-old. My heart was immediately full to bursting with unresolved grief. The vast empty space all around me ignited the pain and loneliness that I had felt then and had kept buried deep inside me ever since.

In 1949, in my Northern English working class culture, and still in the aftermath of the Second World War when almost every family in the land had lost at least one and often more loved ones, grief and bereavement were swept aside by the everyday struggle for survival. A child's feelings were usually not considered. I know mine weren't.

As I walked in this wilderness I clearly remembered the day that my mother died. As soon as I had finished my school lunch my teacher had told me to run home as my daddy wanted to see me. When I entered the back door my father was leaning on the high mantelshelf above the fireplace, resting his head on his arm and crying. My daddy crying; my daddy who had been a big brave soldier and fought in the war – crying? He turned when he heard me shut the door.

'Oh love – come here.'

He hunkered down on his haunches, put his arms around me and held me tight.

'Your poor mum died this morning.'

His body shook with uncontrolled sobs. I cried with him, not so much about my mother dying, because the enormity and the reality of that didn't fully register, but from the shock and surprise of seeing my father in such a distressed and distraught state.

I went back to school for the afternoon session full of bewilderment and helplessness. Those same feelings that had been repressed for sixty years now overtook me. My body was racked with sobs and tears streamed down my face as I wept uncontrollably. I was the lost and lonely ten-year-old child in the head and heart of the lost and lonely seventy-year-old pilgrim. My grief and sense of loss knew no bounds.

Suddenly, for the first time on my pilgrimage I became aware of my feet hurting. Each step felt an agony. I tried to walk on, still blinded by my tears, but there was nothing else for it but to take off my boots to see what the problem was.

I sat down by the wayside - bereft.

As I removed my bloodstained socks three toe nails came away on my left foot, the one with the replacement joint. Another wave of loss and sorrow swept over me.

I sat there on the ground rocking and crying like I had never cried in my life before. Tears flowed non-stop, my nose joined in the flood, snot and teardrops cascaded over and dripped from my chin. Struggling to find a dry tissue

I looked around me. Not another living soul in sight – I could have been alone in the world.

I have no idea how long I sat there, but gradually, so so slowly, my emotions settled down. I managed to tend to my feet, massaging them with lavender-scented foot cream. The rhythmic actions and smell of lavender lulled my soul.

I found a pair of unused socks at the bottom of my rucksack and the very act of putting these on seemed to signify a new start, a new beginning.

The vast emptiness of the landscape seemed to give me comfort, reinforcing in me the fact that in almost my entire life I have stood alone, on my own two feet.

Suddenly my chest swelled with pride as I thought of all the things I had achieved in life.

Feeling light-hearted and full of happiness, even though my feet were killing me, I set off again. Slowly and tentatively I managed the three or four kilometres to the small town of Redicilla del Camino, where I hobbled into the first bar I came to and asked for a cup of tea. No tea - sorry! I was told, so I ordered brandy and coffee instead. At the back of the bar was a small poster of a figure with a "smiley" face and FELICES CRISES blazoned across his chest.

'Que crisis?' I asked.

The bartender raised her right hand and rubbed her thumb and forefinger together. Emphatically she pronounced 'FINANCIAL'.

'No! No! No crisis financial,' I replied. 'The crisis is with my feet! She didn't think that was very funny and turned back for another drag on her cigarette. She ignored me for the rest of my stay!

Somewhat restored by the brandy and coffee, I set off again on my lonely road. My feeling of euphoria and self-belief soon evaporated as I trudged on. Again there was no other person around.

Suddenly the sky was filled with the sound of birdsong from hundreds of skylarks, flying so high that they were invisible to me. The sheer magnitude and beauty of nature washed over me and once more I dissolved into floods of tears. I often struggle with my faith and my belief in God, but it seemed as if He was telling me that I wasn't really on my own. I did get help now and then along the way. Somewhere a competitive cuckoo croaked his raucous song and broke my reverie. I lifted my eyes to look for the cheeky invader and saw him nonchalantly eying me from the branch of a nearby tree.

'And you can bloody well shut up, as well!' I told him.

I managed to walk the next three kilometres to Viloria de Riojo, the village alleged to be the birthplace of Santo Domingo de la Calzada. The church of the Asuncion de Nuestra Señora is said to contain the Romanesque font where the engineer saint was baptised, and later built a bridge, hospital, and hotel in the municipality, for pilgrims. As I hadn't managed to visit the cathedral dedicated to his name I thought I would spend a few minutes in quiet contemplation in the little church, but it was locked!

I was too emotionally and physically exhausted to walk any further, so I knocked on the door of a private hostel, run by a couple named Acacio and Orrietta.

Acacio is from South America and a friend of the renowned Brazilian lyricist and novelist, Paulo Coelho, author of The Alchemist. Acacio told me that Paulo stayed with them when he made his pilgrimage.

Acacio's wife, Orrietta, is Italian.

It was she who opened the door and welcomed me with a huge hug, as if I was a long lost relative. I am not sure what she made of my red and swollen eyes. She made tea and we sat together and talked about the beautiful rustic home that they have made. It was like a "time-warp", a combination of '60s and '70s hippy styling and South American Inca influence. The whole was a simple, new age, comforting haven for me.

No sooner had I started to tell Orrietta about my traumatic day, than the flood gates opened again. She held me in a close and warm embrace until my sobs subsided and a calmness seemed to spread from her and envelop me - body and soul.

Suddenly I felt desperately tired.

Orrietta showed me to my bed and helped me lay out my sleeping-bag and night things.

Emotionally drained and physically exhausted I removed my boots and dropped on to the bed for a moment's rest. Two hours later Orrietta gently shook me awake and invited me to join her and Acacio for supper.

I was the only pilgrim.

The meal was easy and relaxed, rice and lentils in a stew, and salads – new age hippy food to match the new age hippy ambience.

I was tired and emotionally fragile; desperately needing to sleep I was in bed before nine-o'clock. My eyes felt so terribly sore and swollen from all the crying that it was a relief to close them. In a very motherly way Oriette tucked me in with extra blankets and sat and stroked my brow. I was asleep in minutes and hardly moved until 7.30 a.m. This is the longest spell of unbroken sleep I have had for years – six hours being my usual amount at home.

After a breakfast of fruit and cereal I felt ready for the road again, but not before I had decided to leave my crocheted cloche hat, complete with scallop shell (that I had made but never worn) and a hair band that I had never used.

Orrietta had a big box of pilgrim "discards" (it was heartening to know that I was not the only one to bring along extra useless things.) She offered the box for me to see if there was anything in it I might need. I thanked her, but decided that I too was only in "discard" mode.

VILORIA DE LA RIOJA to VILLAFRANCA MONTES DE OCA

Wednesday 1st April 2009 (7th day of walking)

ALL FOOLS DAY- in England!
Count me in!
What kind of fool am I to be doing this - at my age?
Why am I on this lonely road?
Questions, questions - questions running round in my head, but no answers.
Orietta, her lovely open face and bright blue eyes full of compassion, had made me a cup of tea. She had fussed about helping me pack up my rucksack in such a sweet and motherly fashion that she triggered another Niagara of tears.
I quickly hugged her good bye.
I needed to be alone.
The weather was bright and chilly at 7.00 a.m. – just perfect for walking. I had planned to have some moments

of quiet contemplation in the little church, but being so emotionally fragile and weepy I decided just to walk on, rather than meet other communicants.

Solitary walking, memories and questions rolling around and around in my head sent me into a reverie from whence I soon dropped into deep despair. Awash with more floods of tears I realised my life-long suppressed need for mothering – for someone to take care of me . . . a need that I had often hidden behind a brittle façade of brusque confidence and competence.

The shards of grief constantly punctured my mind to reveal yet more long hidden memories, and were overwhelming.

As I walked on I realised, and - what's more - gradually understood, why I had worried, fretted and feared for so many years that I might die young and leave my own three children motherless. How greatly relieved I had been as I saw each one of them passing their childhood and adolescent milestones and move on into adulthood and maturity. How I had supported them through their times of disappointments and set-backs and rejoiced with them over their triumphs and achievements. I thought of how I had struggled to be a good mother and cringed and wept again over the countless mistakes I had made and the times of sadness that I had inadvertently caused my children.

I reflected on the loneliness I had felt on being an almost single parent as my then husband had travelled the world with his job, and my feelings of deep failure and regret when that marriage had ended in divorce. Now estranged from my two oldest children and how not being allowed to share in the lives of my four grandchildren is still heart breaking for me. On and on I trudged, immersed in such reflections of my life history, barely noticing The Way or my surroundings, until eventually I arrived at the little town of Belorado. The place was a hive of activity, with morning shoppers, friends and neighbours meeting and greeting each other or just quietly going about their daily routine. All seemed so normal, so peaceful and untroubled. The very opposite of my own inner turmoil. I stopped for coffee and croissants in a small café and slowly began to relax and enjoy the break, that was until minutes later the horse-faced Dutch girl from Ciraque walked in.

Grateful that my sunglasses hid my swollen eyes, I quickly swallowed my food and drink and left. The last thing I could cope with was another sideways swipe from her caustic tongue. For that matter I couldn't face company or small talk of any sort.

As I set off again the day finally produced clear blue skies. This and the cool fresh air gently wafted from the River Tiron had a wonderfully calming effect on my mind. The little wooded park on the riverside, on the outskirts of the town, was a haven of tranquillity with lazy, laconic birdsong as if the creatures could hardly be bothered to tweet. Their haphazard tunes lifted my spirits and brought a smile to my lips – the first for days.

How apt then that after several more hours of solitary walking, climbing all the way up a wooded hillside I arrived at the Hostal el Pajaro (if my Spanish still serves me well - the Hotel of the Birds) in Villafranca Montes de Oca. What a relief to have a single room, sweet smelling and clean. Having eaten only my rations of dried fruit and nuts all day I was more than ready for my evening meal – what else but fried chicken fillets and salad with a huge glass of blood red Rioja – marvellous!

VILLAFRANCA MONTES DE OCA to BURGOS

Thursday 2nd April 2009 (8th day of walking)

I AWOKE AT 5.30 a.m. from a wonderfully deep and refreshing sleep.
After two emotionally gruelling days my wits were sluggish in coming together, but my heart felt lighter and my body quite supple, pain-free and re-energised – even my feet seemed to be none the worse for the loss of my toe nails.
Soon after 6.00 a.m. I was packed and ready to go.
Dawn was just breaking, the birds clearing their throats ready for their morning choruses as I began the steep but steady climb up through woodland to the peaks of the Oca mountains, and then on to a gentle downward slope through pine forests to San Juan de Ortega.
It took me over four hours of steady plodding upward and onward and then down again on an interminable trek.

It seemed as if the fates were conspiring with me as this was another solitary day for me to enjoy (or endure!) my own company, to put all the emotional turmoil of the last two days into some kind of perspective and gather my "inner" self together again. The amount of self-knowledge that I had gained proved to be a salve to my soul and gave me a large amount of peacefulness and self-acceptance. Maybe it was my imagination but my breathing seemed easier, somehow lighter too!

The albergue I found in Burgos is brand new, ultra-modern, a huge warehouse of a place that sleeps 300; much too big for my liking. At that moment I was averse to communal living. I was quite exhausted after more than eight hours walking and just wanted to rest. The sleeping spaces resembled stacked concrete shoe boxes and could easily be used as a Mediterranean cemetery – chilling, clinical and impersonal, with little sense of community, sharing or intermingling. Suddenly, a swarm of young people invaded the place – a veritable league of nations, chattering and chaffing, pushing and shoving, all very jolly and noisy and quite overpowering for my tired senses.

I found a quiet corner and ate my solitary supper of dried fruits, nuts, liquorice pieces, chocolate and Rowntree's fruit pastilles, all washed down with huge amounts of water.

I felt unutterably alone and lonely, shivery and cold, so at 8.00 p.m. I cleaned my teeth and went to bed in my concrete coffin. I couldn't unwind and sleep so took a sleeping pill, and next thing I knew it was morning.

BURGOS

Friday 3rd April 2009 (9th day of Camino)

COMING ROUND SLOWLY FROM A VERY DEEP SLEEP my senses were bombarded by the smells of aftershave and male deodorants.
The sounds of young men joking and jesting, showering and shaving amid much flicking of towels in a testosterone-fuelled atmosphere was too much for me. Quickly I packed my bag and without even washing my face I checked out of the albergue and headed for a little solitude, some café con leche and a hot croissant with jam and butter sitting outside a café/bar in the cathedral square.
Sitting in the sun, people-watching, day-dreaming and relaxing, I decided to have a couple of days break to recoup my sense of self and try to answer some of the endless questions that continued to roll around in my head.
Stiff from my night on the concrete bed, I climbed slowly up the hill and throwing caution to the winds checked in to a rather grand hotel. The double room, complete with

bath and all facilities, was sheer bliss. The swimming pool in the basement was an unexpected bonus. Dumping my boots, bag, and most of my clothing, dressed in nothing more than the hotel bathrobe and my bra and skimpy pants, I dashed down for a swim.

To be weightless in the gently warm water was a sheer delight, and in an elegant "old lady" style breast-stroke I slowly rid my body of most of its aches and pains.

I decided I wanted to be in Burgos for Palm Sunday, to see the processions to mark the beginning of Holy Week. I needed some more clothes to replace the two lots that I had left behind in washing machines and tumble dryers, and also wanted to explore this famous cathedral city. It somehow just felt right at this juncture for me to take a break from walking – if only for a day or two.

Later, in the Cathedral Square I sat in sunny contemplation on a bench next to a bronze statue of a leper whose disfiguring visual lesions and sores were a reminder of the lesions and sores that afflict us all – externally, internally, emotionally and psychologically. Suddenly, a tourist train "Chu-Chu" stopped in front of me. Dozens of cheerful passenger disembarked and amid their chatter and confusion my quiet reverie was swept away. So, on a whim, I jumped on board to enjoy the child-like thrill of the trip and to learn from the tour guide something of the history and culture of the centuries old city and its monuments.

The guide told us that Burgos was first noted in 884AD when it was a tiny outpost of the burgeoning early Christian empire. It grew slowly and steadily until the 11th century, when it then became the See of a Catholic bishop and the capitol of the Kingdom of Castile. Since then it has always been an important stop for pilgrims on the Way to Santiago.

Apart from its majestic Gothic Cathedral, Burgos is probably most famous for a past resident – El Cid (Rodrigo Diaz de Vivar, 1043-1099), the life and times of whom were highlighted in the spectacular Hollywood film starring the late Charlton Heston.

An imposing statue of El Cid holds pride of place opposite the San Pablo Bridge which is watched over by guardian-like figures, sculpted by the contemporary 20th century artist Joaquin Lucarini, and representing personalities who played a prominent role in the legendary, but real life, saga of El Cid.

After a visit to the post office to repatriate yet more superfluous items from my rucksack – including used pages from my diary and pilgrim guide, unused foot deodorant, glucosamine gel (why did I ever pack this in my first aid kit?) and a pair of still unused socks, I went to the hypermarket to replace bras, pants and leggings that I had "lost" en route, and other goodies to top up my emergency rations of dried fruits, nuts and chocolate - plus a bottle of wine to keep me company in my hotel room.

Back in the Cathedral square I delightedly bumped into Carol, Dan, Gaby, Hannah and Guiseppe again and we chatted a while and arranged to meet for evening mass in the Cathedral.

I spent the afternoon relaxing and reading the book that I had brought with me from home, and had not yet read even a page of! The Dancer - a biography of Rudolph Nureyev, written by Colum McCann, tells a harrowing story of the incredibly deprived childhood, the determination to succeed, the rise to world acclaim, the slide into self-indulgence and debauchery, and finally the long and painful death from Aids of this greatly gifted but psychologically damaged man.

Mass in a side-chapel of the Cathedral that evening was a deeply spiritual experience, and I promised to give myself time to fully explore and enjoy more of this beautiful and sacred building. Dan had joined us for the mass, so the seven of us then went on to a lively bar for dinner. It was boisterous and noisy, but the food was good, and I really enjoyed catching up with my old walking companions. Back in the hotel afterwards, feeling very relaxed and very tired, I became bothered by an itching sensation on my legs and body.

Blast!

In my eagerness to enjoy a swim I had forgotten my tendency to sometimes develop itchy reactions to chemicals in the water of some swimming pools. Now I was paying the price! On top of the "itchies" a couple of blisters on my left foot had become quite painful as well, and looked as if they might even be turning septic.

Double blast!

Still BURGOS

Saturday 4th April 2009 (10th day of Camino)

AFTER A WRETCHED AND RESTLESS NIGHT I made my way to a pharmacy where I managed to buy myself some cream and medication for my "itchies" as well as antibiotics and fresh plasters for my blisters. Back to the hotel to treat "itchies" and feet, and then feeling much more comfortable I set out for my promised trip to the Cathedral.

The first stone of this breathtakingly beautiful Gothic building was laid in 1221, but it took almost two-hundred years to complete. I spent over two hours enjoying its cool tranquillity, marvelling at the vast amounts of gold and stained glass that adorns the walls, ceilings and every side-chapel, nook and cranny of this incredible monument to faith in God. The high point for me was the vault forming an eight point star worked in filigree, and rising on four massive columns above the tombstones of El Cid and his beloved wife Doña Jimena.

After leaving the Cathedral and my eyes adjusting to the bright spring sunshine, I saw a "hole-in-the-wall" cash machine. I topped up my secret stash of euros in my body bag and then took a gentle stroll beside the river. The bliss of not being heavily laden, lightened my heart. I could have wept with the joy of it. Suddenly my heavy bag became a metaphor for my "heavy" life. Putting down the weight and walking free of my past emotional "baggage" as I had over the last few days, felt incredibly liberating. Someone once told me that walking the Camino divides into three stages.

The first stage is the physical one, because we are aware of our bodies, the aches and pains and the discomforts of continuous daily walking and carrying our heavy burdens.

The second is the emotional stage, where we have thinking time, when we experience loneliness and aloneness and discover hidden parts of our inner selves.

The third part is when we have overcome our physical and emotional pain: it is a time of coming to terms with our life – a sense of achievement and a positive feeling of self-worth and confidence. It is only when we are in the light that we can see the dark side! and are more able to travel at ease with ourselves. Hmmm!

Walking back to my hotel I came to the ancient church of St. Nicholas. A bridal party was making its way up the wide sweep of steps towards the beautiful arched doorway. I joined them and sat at the back of the congregation but still fully able to share in the beauty of this age old ceremony of love and commitment. It was a warm and deeply moving experience as I watched the young couple exchanged their marriage vows before their God.

Back in the hotel, feeling restored in mind and spirit, I tended my blistered feet and re-applied the soothing cream to my "itchies" – all the while cursing the person who decided to add chlorine to swimming pools.

BURGOS to VILLABILLA DE BURGOS

Sunday 5th April 2009 - PALM SUNDAY (9th day of walking)

I WOKE EARLY and had a very relaxed and enjoyable breakfast in the elegant dining room under the watchful gaze of the maître de hotel, thinking all the while that it is all very well and commendable being a pilgrim, but creature comforts certainly have a lot going for them! After breakfast I sat in the sunny hotel lounge and finished reading my Nureyev book, leaving it afterwards on a side table along with the newspapers, magazines and other reading materials for future travellers to enjoy.
Back in my room I packed my bag ready for the next stage of my journey. But first I had to go to the Cathedral Square to watch the celebrations of Domingo de Ramos – Palm Sunday - which is massively important in the calendar of the Catholic Church.

Rows of folding chairs had been arranged in front of the cathedral and the area was cordoned off by barriers leaving only a couple of metres round the edge of it for people to stand and watch or for passers-by to get through the throng.

Eleven-o'clock chimed dull and heavy. Music sounded in the distance. Gradually a spectacular procession made its way into the square.

Groups of celebrants peeled off from the main body and sat in their designated areas. Every group had its own particular coloured dresses, gowns and cloaks from white and gold to blue and yellow, with dozens of variants in between, all making an intricate patchwork pattern as each group took its place on the rows of chairs.

I counted more than two dozen different groups, all of them interspersed by musical bands and each adorned in their own individual costume or uniform.

As the chimes of twelve-noon echoed across the square the last of the procession arrived, culminating with the church dignitaries and clerics in their flowing robes and exquisite head-wear and all to the sound of loud "hosannas" as a statue of Jesus on a donkey became the focal point of the proceedings. The heady smell of incense filled the air, wafted by the palms carried by those who walked before the statue.

As the sounds of hosannas faded, a tinkling bell signalled the start of the holy service.

The whole was a wonderfully spiritual and uplifting experience and left me feeling chastened, yet marvelling at the deep and simple faith that is still enjoyed by so many people, not only in Spain, but all around the world. I envy them.

Suddenly, I felt that I had no more part in this ceremony.

I walked away and began the next stage of my pilgrimage, beginning with lunch and a refreshing beer.

The heat of the day was overwhelming, so I walked beside the river to enjoy the last few moments of its peaceful, reflecting beauty before crossing the Puente de Malatos and leaving Burgos behind.

The last week had been cathartic, with a huge emotional clear out.

My heart and my rucksack felt lighter and after two days of respite I felt re-energised and glad to be walking again. But, not too many kilometres later, my feet began to pinch and ache - no doubt from standing for so many hours watching the Palm Sunday celebrations.

I decided that the first refugio I came to would be my resting place for the night.

It seemed that when I needed moments of quiet reflection the Camino always obliged. Today was no exception. I saw no-one apart from a bespectacled, curly-haired young man who gave me a cheery 'Buenas tardes' as he overtook me at a fairly rapid pace.

By mid-afternoon, after only ten tedious kilometres in blazing heat, I reached the tiny hamlet of Villabilla and decided to call it a day.

Everywhere, apart from a dark, smoke-filled bar was closed and shuttered. There was no food available, not even a single tapas, so I had a cool drink and then walked the few yards down the road to where, in the middle of a dry and dusty open space, there stood what looked to be a sports pavilion with a couple of tables and benches in front of it

At one of the tables sat the curly-haired young man who had passed me earlier. He looked, hot, weary and dejected as he sat beside his discarded rucksack. I gave him a friendly, 'Hello, again!' took off my rucksack and jacket and sat on the bench beside him. He said that he had just turned his ankle on a loose stone and needed to rest up for a while.

It is surprising how easily people walking the Camino open up and share their problems – life histories even – to fellow pilgrims.

This man soon told me his name was Paul and that he was French, 34-years-old and a doctor in a busy hospital in Paris. He had given himself sabbatical leave for one month so that he could walk the Camino. He didn't tell me why he wanted to do so but said he was determined to walk about 40 kilometres each day. Today he had started early and had managed more than thirty so far. He rolled up his trouser leg and took off his boot. It was obvious that his ankle was at least sprained and swelling rapidly. I dug in my bag for an elastic bandage and a couple of safety pins. There was a water tap on the side wall of the building so I soaked the bandage in cold water and strapped up his ankle. My Girl Guide first aid badge of 60 years ago had finally come in handy!

Minutes later a statuesque, at least five-feet-ten-inches young woman joined us. She was truly beautiful in a Nordic way with long, thick, curly blonde hair, startlingly blue eyes and a clear, smooth, honey-toned complexion with just the slightest trace of rosy cheeks. She looked truly stunning. Slipping off her rucksack and dumping it on a bench she introduced herself as Sara and told us she was from Sweden.

No sooner had we exchanged names and begun to resettle than another pilgrim shambled into the village and instinctively came across to join us at our table. He introduced himself as André from the Czech Republic. He looked as if he had just tumbled off a 1960's hippie trail with his straggly beard and long plaited and beaded hair and dozens of leather bracelets and beaded bangles which rattled, jingled and jangled around each of his wrists. Whilst we were still shaking hands and shuffling into comfortable places around the table a little roly-poly man ambled up to the big double doors of the building, shook a large bunch of keys, then with hugely exaggerated movements opened one of the doors - all of this without even acknowledging that any of us were there. As he entered the building Sara went after him and in halting Spanish asked what the refugio had to offer. His rapid fire reply was easy to understand: 'Tenemos las camas, pero no tiene comida; hay solo dos servicios y dos duchas, con aqua frio. Dos euros.' Basically, there were beds available but no food or cooking facilities, two toilets, two showers with only cold water. All this for just two euros per person per night? Bargain!

From the sublime surroundings of my hotel in Burgos I was now faced with the ridiculous situation of this most basic or primitive places to spend the night.
The day was still baking hot and after swift deliberation we decided that none of us felt like moving on. We checked in and made up our beds, then as there was nowhere to sit inside we gathered around the outside table again.
What to do about food?
I emptied the contents of my emergency rations bag on to the table – dried apricots, walnuts, almonds, two bars of dark chocolate, a small string bag of a dozen little red-waxed Bon-Bell cheeses, and a packet of savoury biscuits. Sara contributed a couple of bread rolls and a few inches of spicy chorizo sausage.
Paul had a tin of tuna fish and two more bread rolls.
André shuffled off to the bar and soon came back with two

bottles of wine and some bags of crisps. What a feast and what a memorable evening. We sat around and nibbled and drank and talked and talked and talked.

The topics of conversation ranged from euthanasia – André was point blank against it; abortion, no ifs ands or buts, André was totally against this too; the state of the world, the state of the European Community, world finances and the world banking systems, and - again - André contentiously appeared to hold a strongly principled and moral attitude on everything. His input usually had a hopelessly negative slant, except when it came to the use of alcohol and drugs. I couldn't quite make out if his stance and opinions were driven by religious ideals, total unrealistic idealism, or just plain bloody mindedness! I wanted to ask his opinion on shared food and drink, but said nothing.

Paul, the young French doctor was a very quiet, unassuming man but at the same time extremely pragmatic in his arguments. He told us he had reached a crossroads in his private and professional life. He was walking the Camino to give himself space to think through what could be the pros and cons of his decisions.

Three young Spanish pilgrims then arrived and asked if there was room for them to spend the night, but when we told them how basic the facilities were they decided to carry on to the next refugio.

Sara was largely quiet and pensive, until the discussion turned to drink and drugs. She spoke of her chaotic childhood in Sweden where both of her parents had had multiple partners, had abused drugs and alcohol and had given little thought to their more than a dozen children from their ever-changing relationships. She admitted that she had made her peace (a little) with her father as he had been more stable for the last four or five years. She said that he no longer used drugs or alcohol, although this was because he was now slowly dying with severe and serious health complications as a direct result of his previous addictions. Sara confessed that she could not bear to be in the same room as her mother and this troubled her greatly. She told us she was now twenty-eight-years-old and hoped that as she made her pilgrimage she would be able to find it in her heart to forgive her mother, 'for giving me such a crap childhood.' She said that her need to address these issues was because of her wonderful and loving boyfriend who desperately wanted to share his life with her, marry her and raise a family together. Sara was keen to do this but was terrified in case she wasn't good enough and ended up just like her mother. She confessed that her emotional baggage was crushing her ability to think rationally. Her boyfriend had promised to be in Santiago to meet her and to discover what decisions she had made. I largely just listened, really enjoying the lively energy of these young adults.

The sun had gone down and the air had turned quite chilly before we packed away the few bits left over from our alfresco meal and got ourselves sorted and into bed. Although my head was full of all the topics that had been aired I was soon snuggled up in my sleeping-bag and fast asleep.

VILLABILLA DE BURGOS to HONTANAS

Monday 6th April 2009 (10th day of walking)

I WAS AWAKE BEFORE 7.00 a.m. to the sound of the other pilgrims shuffling about and packing their bags. The men left almost immediately.
Sara said she would wait and walk with me for a while. I didn't fancy taking a cold shower so after only washing my hands and face and a quick brush of my teeth I was soon packed and ready to go again.
For almost three kilometres Sara poured out more of her deeply intimate childhood pain and anguish, while I silently marvelled at the inner strength that had helped her to survive such traumas.

The smell of freshly brewed coffee and cooking food drew us to the open door of a small café/bar. As we entered, the three Spanish pilgrims we had re-directed last night, clattered down from upstairs. They had spent the night there and thanked us profusely for sending them away from the austere accommodation at Villabilla. They left us with cheerful farewells and Sara and I enjoyed a breakfast of coffee and hot, home-cooked tortilla. Delicious!
Before leaving this little place, called Tardajos, and its 950 inhabitants, I stocked up my emergency rations at the village store.
Five minutes further along the road Sara stopped, gave me a big hug and said she now needed to be alone. She went off, striding like a Valkyrie, with her mass of golden curls flowing behind her.
Alone again I reflected on all those whom I had already met on the Way and who had danced off to their different beats. It seemed to me that pilgrim walking styles often reflect their states of mind whilst mine, initially, was and is, largely dictated by the weight of my backpack.

In a sunny square, in the tiny village of Hornillas, I came across the three Spanish pilgrims again. They were in playful mood, all sporting red plastic noses. They beckoned me to join them, introducing themselves as Olga, a social worker and laughter therapist – hence the red noses – Lara, and Miguel. They invited me to share in the fun. They all spoke impeccable English and were eager to practice on a "native" speaker. Olga slipped a red nose on me and for almost half an hour we laughed and joked there in the village square before setting off walking again. The youngsters walked at my pace and were happy to be using their English language skills. They were full of such energy and zest for life that it was quite infectious and lifted my spirits enormously. The women told me they were from Barcelona. Miguel said he was from Vianna. As we walked they explained that they had met four years ago, at Saint-Jean-Pied-de-Port as complete strangers and had walked together for Holy Week and ended up firm friends. They had enjoyed each other's company so much that they arranged to meet the next year for Holy Week to continue their pilgrimage, intending to complete the Way with a special few days walking, ending on 25th July, the day of St. James, 2010, which is a Holy Year – this because the Saint's day falls on a Sunday.

Miguel was gentle, very caring and solicitous of my well-being.

He didn't offer to carry my bag though!

We talked about the church of Santa Maria in Vianna and its links with Cesar Borgia. Lara asked questions about England and London and about where I lived and my family. When I told her that I was seventy-years-old she stopped in her tracks, her jaw dropping in amazement. She told me that her grandmother was seventy but she could no longer walk, adding wistfully that she wished her grandmother was like me.

Their questions were unending, until Miguel asked if I liked the Beatles.

I told him Yes.

Did I know any of their songs?

Yes again.

We started off with Yellow Submarine, singing lustily at the tops off our voices, then on to She Loves You and on through the entire Beatles song book with repeats of particular favourites, stopping only for quick drink and refreshment breaks.

We ambled in to Hontanas just after 3.30 p.m.- over eight hours on the road! I felt utterly exhausted and yet at the same time totally exhilarated after such a very happy and light-hearted day in such exuberant young company. We booked into a refugio which was above a bar run by a genial, grizzly, over-weight, middle-aged Spaniard who really fancied himself and flirted with all the females. I was too tired to care!

I staggered up the stairs to the bedrooms above the bar and flopped on to my allotted bed where I fell fast asleep without even removing my jacket.

An hour later, revived by my "nap" and a welcome hot shower, I joined a huge crowd of rowdy pilgrims that had gathered in the bar downstairs. I ordered a coffee and sat on the periphery of the group listening to their banter. The teasing, leg-pulling and joshing was hilarious as the group consisted of a Frenchman from Marseilles, a Canadian from Montreal, a Scandinavian man called Odd, a German woman from Berlin, three or four other men from countries that I couldn't identify from the conversation, my three young Spanish friends, and a Scot from Glasgow accompanied by his fourteen-year-old grandson who he was telling all and sundry suffered from Attention Deficit Hyperactivity Disorder (ADHD). Apparently he was the oldest of three children and his mother could not cope during the school holidays, so grandfather had offered to take the boy off on a holiday. He failed to tell the lad that he would be walking twenty or more miles each day. The grandfather's thinking was that he would not desist or resist when he was in a strange country and so far away from home. It transpired that they had been walking for several days and the boy was enjoying the daily challenge and not causing any problems for the grandfather at all. Ergo - Result!

Soon the food arrived and was a veritable feast of salads, ox-tail stew, fish dishes and even a selection of vegetarian treats, all expertly cooked and tastefully served with freshly baked bread to soak up the sauces and local wines that flowed in abundance. The atmosphere was full of friendly chat and laughter – all in English (or translated into English where necessary.) It was the perfect end to a wonderful day and I went to bed in the mellowest frame of mind that I had enjoyed in years.

I have since read in reviews and heard in comments that this is a less than salubrious refugio – in fact it is reported to be positively gruesome and that the "inn-keeper" is a pestering Lothario. I must have found it on a rare night of cleanliness and good cooking, with the innkeeper so far outnumbered by virile young men that he didn't even bother any of the females. Perhaps, too, his wife was at home!

HONTANAS to FROMISTA

Tuesday 7th April 2009 (11th day of walking)

THE SCUFFLING SOUNDS of pilgrims packing roused me from a deep sleep.
I looked at my watch, it was only 6.30 a.m.
There was a weak dawn light in the room and I could see that most of the beds were already empty.
Gradually, my wits reassembled and in less than half-an-hour I too was ready and off on the road again.
The morning air was fresh and clear with a gentle warming breeze. Walking steadily on an easy, largely downhill track, I was soon surrounded by a multitude of songbirds. The sweetness of the music from their tiny throats was punctuated by the occasional wing flap and rattle of storks as they made their graceful way across the sky. Life felt very good that morning, all seemed right in my world and my solitary progress was quite comforting.

Five miles or so along the way and the smell of freshly baked bread and coffee greeted me as I entered the tiny town of Castrojeriz.

The Scandinavian man from last night's company seemed lost in reverie over his breakfast as he sat in the sunshine outside a small café. He looked up, caught my eye and beckoned me to join him.

Moments later, Margueretta, the woman from Berlin, one of those also in our company last night, strolled into the village and came and sat with us as well.

Breakfast of newly baked bread with melting butter and strawberry jam was sensational, and after two cups of milky coffee I was feeling decidedly mellow and relaxed. We chatted and enjoyed the early morning sunshine.

Margueretta told us that she was a teacher of English in Berlin and had decided to spend two weeks of her Easter vacation walking part of the Camino. She said it was simply to escape the hassle of city life for a while, but she had not expected so much inner turmoil or emotional upheaval.

Odd - which was the abbreviation for some long and virtually unpronounceable Scandinavian name, was a very quiet and contained man, and had the sharpest and bluest eyes I had ever seen - listened the while with an attentive and encouraging manner, which was both charming and beguiling. I liked him immediately.

We bought fresh bread rolls, cheese and tomatoes for lunch. I topped up my water bottle, then we three set off and walked together in quiet camaraderie for a couple of kilometres, until the trail became a steady climb up the Mosterales hill and I was soon left behind.

I would have liked to have lingered in and explored Castrojez, a town built by the Romans, with a wealth of interesting and important historical and ancient buildings.

However, I just added it to my ever-growing mental list of Camino towns that I would re-visit at some other time. The day was deliciously spring-like with soft, gentle breezes, warm sunshine and perfect for walking. Alone again, I enjoyed just being at one with nature, high on the Meseta, reflecting on the spectacular landscape, probably the most beautiful that I had seen so far.

As I neared the village of Itero de la Vega a way mark told me I was now leaving the Province of Burgos and crossing into Palencia. This lifted my heart and spirits, it being a tangible sign that I was making progress and would soon be half-way to Santiago.

I saw few other pilgrims until finally I trudged into Fromista after more than eight hours walking and having covered an incredible forty-plus kilometres.

The albergue Estrella de Camino was bright and modern, clean, and buzzing with pilgrim chatter. I met Carol (the ex-nun from Canada) and Gaby the garrulous Australian who were both as friendly and welcoming as ever. We chatted for a while then I made up my bed, had a shower and took a drink out into the tiny courtyard. There, to my joy, were my three young Spanish friends from the day before. We greeted each other with big hugs, like long lost family members. They were enjoying the warm afternoon sunshine and attending to each other's feet. Lara, short, curvy, cuddly and incredibly giving, insisted on massaging my feet with a wonderful rose-scented cream. Who was I to resist or desist?

The warm sunshine, gentle massage and heady smell of the cream lulled me into a relaxed and peaceful reverie until a huge, jovial Spaniard joined us. He was well over six-feet tall and must have weighed two-hundred-and-eighty-pounds if he was an ounce. He introduced himself as Miguel Angelo. He and my three young friends engaged in rapid Spanish conversation and between them it was decided that if we four gave him three euros each he would shop for and cook our evening meal for us. Again - no resistance from me, I was too tired to be bothered, and quite cheerfully passed over my contribution and continued to enjoy the late afternoon sun in the courtyard happily chatting with my fellow pilgrims.

Miguel's meal was totally Spanish and totally tasty.

We started with a dish of lentils, heavily laced with garlic and herbs, accompanied by fresh crusty bread which was scrumptious. Next we had a tortilla with a side-salad and huge jugs of fruit-filled sangria.

Whatever else, Miguel Angelo could certainly cook!

Olga told me that he was a "professional" pilgrim and that he spent his entire life walking The Way. I couldn't understand how someone could spend his life walking miles each day and still be so overweight. But what do I know? I said nothing and just enjoyed the wonderfully friendly evening in delightfully good company.

There wasn't a bed big enough for Miguel Angelo so the hostelero put two mattresses side by side on the floor for him. His contented snores suggested that he was perfectly happy with this arrangement. I wondered how he would get his huge bulk back on to his feet again, but I needn't have worried; next morning he was up and gone before anyone else was awake.

FROMISTA to CARRION DE LOS CONDES

Wednesday 8th April 2009 (12th day of walking)

I MADE A LEISURELY START TO THE DAY along a fairly straight gravel path that seemed endless.
I walked alone until I reached Villalcazar de Sirga, where a jolly bunch of pilgrims, including my three young Spanish friends, were enjoying a hearty lunch of fried eggs, serrano ham and thick country bread. I joined in and salivated over the best "dipping-in-egg" that I had tasted in a long while.
It was another balmy, soft and warm spring day. We all walked on together, chatting and joking in happy camaraderie, to Carrion de los Condes, and booked into the Monasterio de Santa Clara. We had completed only 20 kilometres, but after our long hike of yesterday it seemed like more than enough.

It was still fairly early in the afternoon so Lara, Olga, Miguel and I, joined by two Englishmen, Chris and his father John, strolled down to explore the town and riverside area.

The family resemblance between the two men was striking. Chris was well over six-feet tall, about 30-years-old, a sports teacher with an incredibly tanned, toned and honed body. John, his father, had the same cornflower blue eyes, blonde hair and big frame as his son, but his face was grey and gaunt and his body skeletally thin, ravaged by the aggressive cancer that was slowly killing him.

We found a tranquil place in the Parque el Eden beside the quietly flowing river.

Olga, tall and stately yet gently calm and composed led us, in perfect English, through an incredible session of her laughter therapy.

Far from it being a "laugh" it was a deeply moving and thought-provoking experience.

Yes, we laughed and we cried and we meditated, enjoying the peacefulness of being at one with nature, lying on the soft grass aware of the sounds of the nearby rippling river, the occasional late afternoon tweet of a restless bird or two, the happy chatter of children playing in a distant part of the park and the smells of flowers and blossom wafting on a gentle breeze whilst we relaxed in the warm spring sunshine. We ended the session in a gleeful group hug that was strangely comforting.

It was a beautiful experience, and a hugely meaningful one for Chris and John, who shared some incredibly tender, loving moments.

We walked into the town together and enjoyed a meal in a restaurant in the main square before watching the local Semana Santa procession. Again I was touched by the deep faith so many Spanish people share during Holy Week.

After a couple of beers in a down-town bar, we ambled back to the convent in a very mellow mood.

Sadly, my night-time experience was far from "mellow". I had, possibly, one of the world's noisiest snorers in the bunk next to me and his racket made unbroken sleep virtually impossible. To crown it all, young Alistair, the Scottish boy with ADHD, fell off the top bunk opposite me and made such a commotion the entire dormitory was roused. What with the countless grumbles, the rampant snorer and Alistair's moans I had very little sleep - I don't think anyone else had much that night either!

CARRION DE LOS CONDES to SAHAGUN

Thursday April 9th 2009 (13th day of walking)

THIS PROVED to be an extremely gruelling walk. What looked to be a long, straight, road actually went uphill and downhill, uphill and downhill, relentlessly straining my left ankle and causing severe pain in my "bad" foot. Not steep hills, just enough incline to stretch and pull muscles and tendons in parts of my legs that I didn't know had tendons. There were no trees or buildings, in fact no landmarks at all to break the monotony of endlessly identical wheat fields on either side of the path. No other pilgrims were visible ahead or behind me and for the first time on The Way I was beginning to feel afraid. My guide book clearly stated that the village of Calzadilla de la Cueza was only ten miles from Carrion and yet after nearly three hours of punishing walking on legs and feet that screamed in pain and ached to rest, there was no sign of it on the horizon. Panic swept through me, perhaps I was lost again. I began another of my internal arguments.

Of course I'm not lost. There are no deviations from the track.

But what if I missed a side-turning, an off-shoot without noticing it?

Rational me and fearful panicky me continued in this vain for what felt like another ten miles of onward plodding, when suddenly, less than a hundred yards away, in yet another incline in the track, the village appeared – like Brigadoon!

Although it was nearly mid-day this tiny village seemed deserted, without a single soul or dog on the street. I went into the only hotel, a dark and gloomy place, and had a coffee. The whole area felt uncomfortably disturbing.

Despite my painful legs, I just had to move on.

The trail crossed the main road to Sahagun.

I decided to walk on this road, thinking it would be easier on my feet than the unevenness of the stones and gravel of the trail.

It was, but only marginally.

My legs and feet were in such a bad way that even walking on a feather bed would have been painful. By the time I stumbled into Terradillos de los Templarios I could bear it no longer. The hostel was open and the receptionist kindly called a taxi to take me to Sahagun. By this time I hated the solitude of the Camino, hated the boring countryside, hated myself for needlessly punishing my body - I just hated the whole idea of a pilgrimage, and had to get back into some kind of civilisation.

When I checked into the Albergue Vitorias in Sahagun, there was already a group of "walking-wounded" there, gathered round a table sharing a late lunch and a couple of bottles of wine. They beckoned me to join them and I gladly hobbled over to the proffered seat and a glass of potent red Rioja. Cheese, ham, bread and tomatoes were pushed down the table for me to take my pick. This was such a welcome relief and distracted me somewhat from the throbbing ache in my now quite badly swollen left ankle.

They proved to be a hearty group and introduced themselves as Andreas (from Venice), blond, curly-haired and cheerful Cornelius (from Germany), Lola, (from Toulouse, and very French) and Steve, the guy from Montreal who I had previously met in Hontanas. All of them were suffering from diverse ailments and we had a lively discussion on the psychological – as well as physical – effects of the Camino. We talked about our various Camino experiences, our hopes and aspirations. Someone produced a well-known Camino poem, in Spanish, of which we made a group Translation.

This is the result:-

Dust, mud, sun and rain
Is the road to Santiago.
Thousands of pilgrims
And over a thousand years
Pilgrim, who calls you?
What hidden force draws you?
Neither the field of stars
Nor the great cathedrals.
It's not sturdy Navarre,
Nor the wine from Rioja
Nor Galician seafood
Nor the fields of Castille.
   Pilgrim, who calls you?
What hidden force draws you?

Neither the people along the way
Nor country customs.
It's not history and culture,
Nor the cockerel in Santo Doming de la Calzada
Nor Gaudi's palace
Nor the castle in Ponferrada
I see it all as I pass along
And it is a joy to see,
But the voice that calls me,
I feel more deeply still.
The force that drives me
The force that draws me
I am unable to explain.
Only he above knows!

Lara, Olga and Miguel arrived at 6.30 p.m. after more than nine hours walking. When Olga saw the state of my ankle she immediately filled a sock with ice cubes from the tiny freezer and wrapped it round the swollen area.
It was agony.
Five minutes later she removed the sock then wrapped a warm woollen scarf round my ankle and foot and put the ice-filled sock back in the freezer. Five minutes of one, then five minutes of the other, repeatedly for almost an hour, helped ease the pain. A long crêpe bandage appeared from somewhere and the offending ankle was expertly strapped up by Olga's gentle hands.
We shared a very tasty garlic-laced soup, made by Steve and Lola, then pasta in a tomato sauce with lashings of grated cheese and - finally - large juicy oranges.
Communal pilgrim food can be a welcome, cheap and healthy option when the cash contributions, preparing, cooking, and washing up are evenly shared.

There was to be a Semana Santa procession in the town centre.

I was loathe to miss the opportunity of seeing true Spanish culture and tradition again so, using my two sticks, I gingerly made my way down the hill and was glad I made the effort to see once more a demonstration of Spanish faith in such a deeply moving and spectacular procession.

Later, enjoying a couple of beers and reflective chat in a quiet bar, Andreas and Cornelius decided to take the train to Leon at 8.00 the next morning. I was encouraged to join them so that I could get expert medical attention for my ankle.

After the previous restless night and the rigours of the day I was glad to tumble in to bed, un-washed, but not in the least bit bothered about "hygiene".

I took a sleeping pill and was "out" in minutes.

My 13th day of walking had certainly been unlucky for me!

SAHGUN to LEON

Friday April 10th 2009 – Good Friday (My 14th day of "travelling")

ALL NIGHT THE PULSING, throbbing pain in my ankle had pierced even my drugged sleep.
As soon as people began emerging from their sleeping-bags and shuffling around I slid out of bed and gingerly tested my weight on my aching leg. I winced with the searing pain but determinedly hobbled slowly up and down the length of my bed space; up and down, back and up, each step an untold agony.

I had to manage.

I had to cope.

I had to walk to the railway station so that I could get to Leon and, hopefully, to at least see a doctor - or better still find an emergency department in a hospital.

Olga, Lara and Miguel each hugged me "good-bye" and promised to see me the next day in Leon.

After they left, and for the first time during my pilgrimage I felt utterly and desperately alone and lonely, both physically and spiritually alone and lonely.

I was bereft.

Hot tears stung the back of my eyes, but I quickly blinked them away, packed up my bed and stowed all my bits and pieces into my rucksack. I just about managed to get my boot on to my left foot but had to leave the lacing slack and loosely tied. With gritted teeth and the aid of my two walking sticks I managed, like an angry old woman, to limp my way down the hill to catch the early train.

Andreas and Cornelius were already there, along with a slim, blonde, young woman who introduced herself as Monica. She told me she had dislocated a knee-cap and had to get to Leon to make travel connections so that she could get back home to Switzerland. To give up after getting so far was a prospect that had not really entered my head (although I had sometimes, albeit fleetingly, thought of it!) Now my body gave an involuntary shudder. I blew out a deep breath. I knew that whatever transpired I really couldn't face going home, no matter how long it took, without finishing my journey. Failure was simply not an option.

The train sped along and from time to time ran parallel to the Camino. I caught wistful glimpses of solitary pilgrims or groups enjoying their shared experience. I offered up a silent prayer: Please let my foot and ankle be strong enough for me to get to Santiago.

We arrived in Leon just after 10.00 a.m.; just in time to see the most incredible Good Friday procession. I learned later that this is one of the biggest Semana Santa celebrations in the whole of Spain. There were dozens of holy catafalques depicting various scenes of the Crucifixion of Jesus and other events of that day. There were numerous marching bands playing soulful dirges and hundreds of hooded penitents - many of them walking in bare feet. It took almost an hour for them all to pass by.

The day was overcast with a leaden grey sky, threatening to rain. A chill wind whistled round the squares and narrow streets adding to the sombre mood.

We decided to find an albergue so that we could shed our rucksacks and then find somewhere to eat. I was desperate to get medical attention for my ankle and foot which were again causing me terrible pain.

We found an albergue down a narrow side-street but it transpired that it was also a Benedictine monastery. Several catafalques were in its courtyard being prepared for the evening procession. It looked like a grim and forbidding place so we made our way to the very big municipal albergue. This seemed a better place, very new and modern and exceptionally clean, with all manner of facilities including internet access and a laundry.

We all checked in, and after leaving my rucksack on my bed I enquired at the reception desk about medical help for my foot and ankle. A taxi was promptly telephoned for and within half-an-hour I was in the hospital being seen by a kindly, elderly doctor who spoke perfect English. She told me to rest my leg as much as possible and gave me a note to enable me to stay in the albergue for two nights – great! She prescribed pain-killers and anti-inflammatory medication and sent me off with her blessing for a safe continuing journey to Santiago.

Back at the albergue Monica, Andreas and Cornelius were still intent on catching up with their email correspondence. I took a double dose of my medication to help the healing kick in more rapidly, then we four walked together to the city centre.

St. Martin's Square was thronged with pilgrims and tourists.

The sun had finally broken through the clouds, bringing a bright cheerfulness with it, and the atmosphere in the square was vibrant. We tried tapas and "limonada" (I think this is a special Spanish Eastertime drink, which I thought to be the equivalent to ordinary lemonade) in three different bars, then a huge falafel which we shared between us, then more "limonada".

By now the afternoon had turned very warm, creating an exciting, festive air with much jostling and laughter between and amongst the crowds of people. But . . .

. . . aha!

I had had no idea that the "limonada" was alcohol fuelled. I was feeling quite lightheaded.

High as a kite actually – and no wonder, with all that "limonada" on top of my medication!

Monica wanted to visit the Cathedral before she went home so I offered to go with her. We stopped at a small pavement café near the Cathedral where we each had huge glasses of thick black coffee, a dish of ice-cream and a fit of the giggles.

I guess we were coming "down" after the large amounts of limonada we had downed.

The contrast from the brightness of the afternoon sunshine in the square to the cool, dark, Gothic splendour of the interior of the cathedral was overwhelming. Over a hundred stained glass windows filtered light and sunrays across its beautiful oak woodwork, so delicately carved by master craftsmen more than seven hundred years ago. The thought of the dedicated stone masons, carpenters and the whole army of medieval workers striving in great faith and dedication to build such an awesome monument to their God reduced me to tears.

So overcome was I by the greatness of it all that I could do no more than sink to my knees and bow my head in silent meditation.

Making my way back to the refugio I became entangled in another procession, and lost sight of Monica. Hobbling along a narrow side-street I became hemmed against the wall by the penitents and a catafalque and only just managed to scramble into a doorway and avoid being crushed to death as they went on their spiritual way, quite oblivious of the English pilgrim standing in such a silly, dangerous place.

Nearing the refugio I became caught up with some kind of police incident. There were three police squad cars and more than a dozen police officers. It turned out to be a severe case of domestic violence. I watched a man being taken away in handcuffs whilst a badly battered, bruised and totally exhausted woman was helped to one of the squad cars by a couple of police-women.

All human life, from the sublime to the ridiculous, abounds in this city.

I finally arrived back at the refugio at eight-thirty, more than twelve hours since I'd started my day on my aching, painful legs and feet. The full effects of the medication and the limonada were now wearing off, so after a quick shower, another dose of my medication and a sleeping pill, I was soon into a deep and peaceful sleep.

LEON

Saturday 11th April 2009 – Easter Saturday

I AWOKE SLOWLY AND LAZILY and marvelled at yet another wonderfully sunny spring day.
This was the 18th day of my trip and I had not had to use my waterproof jacket or trousers even once, let alone my massive waterproof poncho, which is big enough to cover not only me but my oversized rucksack too!
Not having to pack up my bed and bag and get back on the trail gave me a wonderful sense of relief. I gingerly tested my foot and ankle and was pleased to only have pain that caused a slight "wince" rather than the previous full-blown agony.
I ate an Oaty Crunch snack bar and took a dose of my medication, washed down with a swig of water, before getting showered and dressed and ready for breakfast.
Cornelius, Andreas and Monica were busily engaged at the computer station of the albergue, but they decided to join me in a quiet stroll into town to find a place to have our breakfast.

Settled once more in St. Martin's Square, which seemed to be the hub of the city, we enjoyed watching the place gradually come back to life again after all the energy and activity of the night before. No sooner had I started on my coffee, hot croissants and jam than Hannah, Guisseppe, Joseph, Dan, Gaby and Carol walked into the square. After hugs and introductions all round they pulled up tables and chairs and all joined us for breakfast. I told them about my ankle problem and Hannah suggested that I should buy some special sandals like hers, which she had worn from the beginning and hadn't had so much as a blister. It sounded like a good idea. My foot was so badly mangled I was willing to try anything.

After breakfast, Cornelius and Monica left to catch the train to Astorga, their particular Camino journey now over. Andreas decided to explore the rest of the town and the riverside area as well as visit the cathedral. We arranged to meet in the square later for lunch. Hannah and Guiseppe told me that they were going home later that day to help their son on the farm, but were planning to come back to Leon in late September when the harvest was in and the most intense farm work was slowing down. They said they hoped to finish their Camino before the autumn weather became too cold and wintry. I wished them well and hugged them good-bye and decided it was time to go and try to find some "walking" sandals so that my swollen ankle wasn't being aggravated by my boots. The side roads leading off from St. Martin's Square were now thronged with Saturday shoppers, but I soon found a store that in pride of place in their window display had a pair of sandals identical to the ones worn by Hannah. Something told me that I was not the first pilgrim to arrive in Leon in need of a change of footwear!

It was bliss to walk around in the shop in such lightweight, comfortable sandals. I paid for them, put my boots in a bag and went back to the albergue to meet Lara, Olga and Miguel. This was their last day too. They were heading home and promising to meet each other in Leon for the last leg of their trip next year. But, before they left, we decided to have a farewell lunch with several other pilgrims that we had met during the last few days.

Back in St. Martin's Square ten of us gathered round a long table. We were a real league of nations, with Helen from Switzerland and her husband from Peru, Odd from Scandinavia, Lara, Olga and Miguel from Spain, Andreas from Italy, Margit from Germany, Francis from Ireland and me from England. We had an amazing array of traditional Spanish tapas that kept coming to the table in waves, each dish seeming to be more interesting and tastier than the last. The Peruvian insisted on putting 50 euros on the table to cover the wine. So very generous of him – no limonada today, just wonderful Riojas to accompany our feast.

It was the most convivial and heart-warming experience of my trip so far and a great farewell party for my three Spanish friends. I was truly sad when they left to catch their train home and the party broke up. I was amazed when I looked at my watch – we had been round the table for more than three hours.

Some feast!

Some farewell party!

I walked back to the albergue on well-cushioned feet which felt light as air. I was really confident and full of hope about continuing my walk next day.

Gaby, Carol, Joseph and Dan were in the albergue and they invited me to join them for the evening. I dumped my boots on my bed, took a further dose of my medication, which was really working now (although it could have been helped by the copious amounts of alcohol that had been passing my lips!) and went off to watch yet another Semana Santa procession.

The splendour and hundreds of years of tradition behind these pageants is quite humbling, with so many volunteers carrying the catafalques (often 30 or 40 men under each one) accompanied by so many penitents in their hooded outfits, looking like escapees from some sinister purple, black and dark green Klu Klux Klan gathering.

The dozens of women dressed in black, with their heavy lace mantillas, so devout in their faith, graceful and serene, add a particular poignancy to these most deeply religious and spiritual occasions.

Over the past week, watching so many of these scenes in such varied and different towns and villages, all depicting the various stages of the journey of Jesus from wild hosannas on Palm Sunday right on to his death on the cross, has stirred my faith and beliefs and disturbed my thoughts on my religion in particular and world religions in general.

Our dinner that evening was a subdued affair, especially after the afternoon's delight, as Dan and Joseph planned to each make a very early start the next day. Joseph told us he aimed to complete the Camino in the next seven days, so this was probably going to be the last time we saw him as he was in a different alburgue to the rest of us. We wished him love and luck as we said our good-byes, then took a taxi back to the refugio.

My head was swirling from the events of the day so I just had a quick wash, another dose of my medication and a sleeping pill, but even so it was ages before I got off to sleep. Communal living is not really my most favourite way of being. I find the snuffles, snores and farts of those around me most disconcerting and, frankly, quite inhibiting!

LEON to LA CASA DEL CAMINO

Sunday 12th April 2009 – Easter Day (14th day of walking)

THERE WAS A DISTURBANCE in the dormitory at 3.00 a.m. – one pilgrim left and another arrived.
The newcomer turned out to be a young Englishman who took over the still warm bed of the departee.
Despite this interruptive nocturnal occurrence, I was still awake fairly early, feeling refreshed and ready to get back on the trail. However, I was eager to see the final Semana Santa procession. Having witnessed a week of pain and passion, I now wanted to share the triumph of the resurrection.
I took a long, slow shower, washed my hair and felt one hundred percent better than I had when I arrived in Leon two days ago.
Chatting with the newly arrived Englishman, he told me that his Camino journey was a special treat for him as he was planning to go to Germany to run a bar which he intended to call "The Swinging Cymbal". This, apparently,

was the signature tune of his favourite radio disc jockey. I wished him well as he strapped on his minute back pack, donned his "pork-pie" hat and with a cheerful 'adios' went on his way.

I watched the procession which was of breath-taking magnificence, a celebration in white and gold, full of joy and thanksgiving for the resurrection. The music was triumphal and light, which was such a huge contrast to the doleful dirges of the past week. The sheer beauty of it all lifted my spirits to heights that I had not experienced for years.

After this pageant everything else seemed like an anti-climax. I had a quick coffee with Andreas, bade him a swift goodbye and set off on the next stage of my Camino journey alone.

The route out of Leon is dire, almost as bad as the way into Burgos, along a main road through bleak housing estates and grim industrial areas – all seemingly deserted on this holiest of Holy days. I decided to keep walking on the main road rather than chance my ankle on the rougher, stony terrain of the Camino trail.

I had walked about ten or twelve miles when a big blister began troubling me.

So much for Hannah's infallible sandals!

One foot problem almost solved and now another one presents me with a dilemma.

I wondered if this was a sign that I really should give up on this venture.

Another internal discussion slightly distracted me from my discomfort, until I happened to see a building on the opposite side of the road with ALBURGUE emblazoned in huge capital letters all along its roof. I wasn't sure where exactly I was, but I was sure that this alburgue was not in my guide book. I gingerly crossed the road and walked into what, to all intents and purposes, was a deserted market garden with a few tables and chairs scattered about. I eased off my rucksack and sank into a chair – bliss to be off my feet again.

'Señora'?

A quiet female voice shook me out of my reverie.

I looked behind me and saw a tiny, quintessentially Spanish-looking, middle-aged woman walking towards me. In halting English she asked me if I had a problem with my feet.

I nodded.

She asked if I would like a beer.

I nodded again.

She disappeared, only to return a couple of minutes later with an ice-cold beer and a large piece cut from an aloe vera plant.

The beer was as sweet and refreshing as nectar and I drank it down in one full swallow.

The woman pulled up a chair and sat in front of me and removed the sandal and sock from my left foot – the still slightly swollen one - propped my foot on her knee and then squeezed some of the plant gel onto her hands and very gently massaged it into the inflamed and swollen area.

It was wondrously soothing and cooling and I just closed my eyes and relaxed with the warm afternoon sun on my face.

After a few minutes she carefully replaced the sock and sandal on that foot, then proceeded to attend to my other foot. She worked the gel around, gently missing the blistered area. When she had finished she fished a packet of Compeed plasters from her apron pocket, put a huge one over the blister, then very caringly replaced my sock and sandal again. She asked me if I was hungry. I was so overcome by her kindness that I could barely speak, so I did no more than nod and whisper 'Yes'.

She disappeared again and within minutes was back carrying a tray with another glass of beer on it, an omelette and a side-salad as well as a huge chunk of freshly baked, crusty bread. A tear or two of relief and gratitude rolled unbidden down my cheeks. Who can doubt the presence of guardian angels along the Camino?

The food was delicious, the omelette light and runny with soft melted cheese, the salad crisp and fresh – this was exactly what I needed.

I was beginning to feel soothed and very tired.

When I had finished eating, the woman carried my bag and ushered me into a cosy communal room which seemed to serve as kitchen, dining and sitting area. A log stove crackled away at one end of the room, making it pleasantly warm and welcoming. I was the only pilgrim, and after all the activities of Leon I was glad of the peace and quiet.

All this for twelve euros – what a bargain!

I still wasn't sure where I was, but the stamp in my pilgrim passport says:- "La Casa del Camino, floristeria y albergue", but with no name of the town or village - so I am still none the wiser.

But it must be one of the best albergues on the Camino.

ON to SANTA CATALINA DE SOMOZA

Monday 13th April 2009 (15th day of walking)

THIS DAY SEEMED SLIGHTLY SURREAL. I awoke early and was on my way before 7.00 a.m.
With no sign of the woman from yesterday, or any other sign of life for that matter, I just left a little note of "thank you" on my bed. I decided to continue walking on the main thoroughfare and walked for miles and miles, stopping only for the occasional coffee and snack. I never ceased to be amazed at the amount of time I was spending alone and yet I was only infrequently afraid or lonely.
I spoke to no one other than the waiters who served my coffee. That was fine by me. I felt happy with my own company until I was four or five miles from Astorga where I saw a yellow arrow and took a chance on the stony footpath once more.

Whenever I have been alone or feeling even slightly lonely on the Camino I have always felt the presence of birds around me and marvelled at the beauty of wild bird song. Today was no exception.

No sooner was I back on the trail than I was aware of the sweet tones of skylarks trilling away and the harsh chatter of magpies. Then a lone cuckoo joined in and sang for ages. Not for the first time on my trip had a cuckoo serenaded me; maybe it was the same one, following my progress! Anyway, this time I got the message—I must be "cuckoo" doing what I was doing..!

I arrived in Astorga in mid-afternoon, but didn't quite like the feel of the place.

I wandered up to see the Gaudi building I had read so much about in various guide books, intrigued and prepared to be impressed.

This Episcopal Palace, designed in a neo-Gothic style by Gaudi is said to have taken more than twenty years to build. To me it looked like something from Disney World. I was totally unimpressed and chose to give it a miss. I felt the same about Astorga itself, so continued to walk on a while longer.

Five miles further, on a distinctly uphill road, I arrived at Santa Catalina de Somoza.

This village had a warm, soft and welcoming feel. It seemed to encourage me to stay for the night in what I presumed was a fairly newly built bar and albergue.

I showered and changed in pristine surroundings and afterwards had a meal in the bar downstairs.

Again I was the only pilgrim, and as the bar was full of men I didn't fancy engaging in conversation, so just chilled out in my room. I trimmed and filed my toe and fingernails then checked my maps and guide books. I figured it out that I had about 160 more miles to go to

Santiago. I resolved that from now on I am not going to push myself at all. Softly, softly will be my motto. I now realise, and fully understand, that I don't have to prove anything to myself or others ever again. I never ever need to climb another mountain, either physically, spiritually or metaphorically. This was a really comforting thought and a big psychological step forward for me as I have spent most of my life trying to impress others and prove to myself that I am an OK person.

SANTA CATALINA to EL ACEBO

Tuesday 14th April 2009 (16th day of walking)

I HAD SLEPT ONLY FITFULLY AND HAD had a peculiar and disturbing dream.
I awoke full of trepidation and fear to hear an inner voice say, 'Don't stay in Rabanal.'
I don't remember many details of the dream - only that it had to do with strategic battle plans and that I had to find Dan (the American) to protect me. Weird!
I was out of bed at 5.30 a.m., slowly pulled myself together, shook off the anxiety that had been around when I awoke, and was on my way before 6.00 a.m.
Dawn had not yet fully broken.
I walked briskly in the half light, in the fresh chill morning air. The path was a steep uphill climb but, surprisingly, my feet felt good and I made it to El Ganso village in an hour.

An elderly pilgrim sat on the church steps there eating his self-made breakfast. He hailed me with a cheery, 'Buenos dias! and a friendly wave.

This tiny village was still shut and sleeping, with no place to find food or drink so I just had a long drink of water and carried on walking.

The road was incredibly steep but I took my time, softly, softly, no stress or pushing myself, and reached Rabanal before 10.00 a.m.

This was another "must see" place on my Camino list. As a member of the Confraternity of St. James I had followed the progress of the work involved in converting the building into a modern refugio.

It was too early for me to stop walking for the day and spend the night, but I at least wanted to have a look around the place.

The two volunteer hospitaleros were just about to dash down to the market in Astorga, but they kindly showed me around first and stamped my pilgrim passport for me.

I was impressed with what has been achieved and wished that I had planned my route so that I could have spent more time there.

However, I had two large milky coffees and croissants with jam in a small bar opposite the church to raise my energy levels, then refreshed and re-energised continued on what seemed to be an endless uphill slog.

It was while I was on my solitary way that I realised that my huge rucksack was no longer a problem for me. I was now able to carry it with relative ease. Beside the worry of my feet and ankle I suppose the issue of the rucksack had paled into insignificance, or, maybe like a snail I had just become used to bearing the load on my back. Whatever the reason, I was now managing fine.

Foncebadon looked to be the most unwelcoming place on the Camino.

I entered the main street with more than a hint of unease; thinking of Paulo Coelho and his report of his battle with the black dog.

I needn't have worried.

The place was very quiet with not a sight nor sound of a dog to be found.

There was an old car outside what seemed to be a ruined church. A pretty, young woman, probably in her mid-thirties, was taking foodstuffs from the car into the church. A couple of very tall men came out to help her. I walked over to investigate. Well . . .

. . . this ruin of a church turned out to be the refugio - and the two tall men, both Canadians and built like lumberjacks, were the volunteer hospitaleros on the last leg of their two week stint in Foncebadon.

They invited me to join them for an early lunch and I was glad of the chance to have a break, having been on the road for almost six hours.

The church was quite large, with a very high ceiling. It was cold, damp, dusty and without a shred of comfort on offer. Even without the memory of Paulo Coelho's dog-fight I knew that I absolutely did not want to spend the night there.

Much to my surprise, the old man that I had seen breakfasting in El Ganso was already in the church and joined with us for lunch. It was simple and basic fare, just vegetable soup, bread and cheese but the conversation was fun and hearty.

The young woman introduced herself as Anna. She told me she was from Poland and had spent the last two weeks as hospitalera in El Acebo. This was her last day as she was moving on the following morning to take charge of the enormous albergue at Ponferrada.

The old man sat quietly, eating but not joining in the conversation. His fingers were busy, twisting and dancing like a pair of agitated butterflies. I thought he had some kind of nervous affliction, but then after a few minutes he tapped me on the arm and presented me with a dear little rosary that he had been fashioning out of beads and different coloured wires. I was deeply moved by this gift, and felt slightly silly that I had thought his flying fingers were due to some kind of cerebral glitch!

I decided that I would aim to reach El Acebo for my next overnight stay.

I gave the hospitaleros a couple of euros for my lunch, thanked them for their hospitality and went with Anna the two kilometres to the Cruz de Ferro (the Iron Cross). This is a famous landmark on the Camino. It was originally erected to help pilgrims find their way across the mountains. So many experienced pilgrims at CSJ meetings in London had told me about the tradition of pilgrims taking a stone from home to add

to the massive cairn that had built up over the years around the base of the tall wooden pole with its small metal cross on the top.

Legend has it that this is where pilgrims have symbolically shed their inner, psychological burdens for more than a thousand years.

I had brought with me a little flint stone from the beach at my home in Eastbourne, and decided to insert it into one of the long vertical splits in the wooden pole.

Anna took several photographs of me in action, and as the afternoon was bright and clear she also took a few pictures of the wonderful views across the valley, promising to send them home for me via email so that my husband could forward them to our friends, relatives and the local newspaper, all of whom were monitoring my progress.

The four or five miles to El Acebo were largely downhill. By the time I arrived at the albergue I had travelled about eighteen miles or so in roughly ten hours! This was definitely a snail pace, but absolutely in line with my new "softly-softly" approach to my Camino progress.
I was amazed to arrive at the albergue to find the old man from earlier in the day was already there, but I never saw him pass me on the road. That was twice he had overtaken me without my noticing. Perhaps he knew of some shortcuts!
As soon as the sun went down, the evening turned very cold; little wonder, as according to my guide book we were high in the mountains and over 1,450 metres above sea level. Another gem from the guide book states that this is the highest point of the entire Camino. However, it also adds a grim warning that it is far from downhill all the way to Santiago!
The albergue was very rustic, reminiscent of the bunkhouses in films of cowboys in the wild west, but it was clean, cosy and warm, with a friendly bunch of pilgrims. Two Belgian women, a mother and daughter, volunteered to cook a communal meal of spaghetti and salad for everyone and we all ate together around a long, scrubbed pine table.
The Belgian daughter told us that her father had died thirteen years ago and that every year since then her mother had walked the Camino in his memory. The five daughters didn't want their mother to walk alone so each of them walked for a week or so with her, swapping shifts as it were, at pre-arranged strategic points along the way. Amazing!

After our meal the Belgians went to bed and the rest of us repaired to the kitchen where the old man washed up the dishes and I dried. We spent an hilarious hour, speaking in broken English and halting Spanish, sharing anecdotes of our individual Camino adventures. The old man turned out to be quite a character and wonderfully entertaining.

When everyone had gone to bed Anna and I sat alone by the heater having a final night-cap cup of English tea. She told me that when she had finished her stint as a warden in Ponferrada she intended to walk her own Camino in memory of her seventeen-year-old son who had recently been killed in a motor car accident.

I have found the untold sadness in the hearts and stories of some of the pilgrims that I have met to be profoundly moving.

Anna gave me extra blankets, one to go under my sleeping-bag and one to go over me to ward off the cold in the middle of the night. As I lay there snuggled up, cosy and warm I shed a few silent tears as my mind went over the experiences of a very long and very interesting day. Here and there I had felt a touch of magic, or maybe the guardian angels of the Camino had been at work again!

EL ACEBO to PONFERRADA

Wednesday 15th April 2009 (17th day of walking)

I AWOKE UNBELIEVABLY LATE (8.00 a.m.!) after a deep and refreshing sleep.
Everyone had already left the refugio, except Anna, preparing for her hand-over to the next hostalero.
We shared a coffee and toast before I packed up my bed and bag ready for the next stage of my journey.
Ponferrada sits 17 kilometres below El Acebo, down an often dangerously steep route.
But on this, another gloriously bright and sunny spring morning, the views were breathtaking.
When I arrived at the town's municipal albergue it was closed and a large group of pilgrims were hanging around impatiently waiting for the hospitaleros to open the doors.
I didn't feel like standing around so I walked on to look for the 12th Century castle of the Knight Templars that I had read so much about in my preparations for this

pilgrimage – but that, too, was closed! Obviously, long lunches and siestas still rule in rural Spain.

By the time I found a supermarket that was open, stocked up on foodstuffs and walked back to the albergue, its doors were open and dozens of walk-weary pilgrims were shuffling their way towards the reception desk to book in and get their pilgrim passports stamped.

The albergue is a massive, fairly new building with two hundred bed spaces and very noisy, with sounds echoing and bouncing off its cement walls.

Luckily I managed to get myself a bottom bunk and quickly unpacked my sleeping-bag, stowing my rucksack under the bunk. After tucking in to a tasty snack from my fresh provisions, ham and cheese in a half-baguette with sliced tomato on the side, I decided to go off once more to explore the town.

Ponferrada is definitely not a place of beauty.

The new parts are mostly nondescript blocks of apartments and supermarkets that can be seen in any modern European city.

The old town area, however, is full of history and very interesting. I managed to get into the "now open for business" castle, town hall and tourist office and collect leaflets and information sheets and get my pilgrim passport stamped by officials in all three places!

Back at the albergue I saw Anna ensconced and harassed behind the reception desk. She said she felt quite out of her depth. Pilgrims were teeming into the place like swarms of locusts. I made her a cup of tea and sat beside her for a while, if only to offer moral support!

Later I browsed through all the information leaflets that I had collected in Leon and Ponferrada, before parcelling them up and sending them off to one of my grandsons who was maintaining a frieze of "granny's pilgrimage" around his bedroom walls.

PONFERRADA to RUITELAN

Thursday 16th April 2009 (18th day of walking)

I AWOKE JUST AFTER 6.00 a.m. to pandemonium, the clatter and chatter of people messing about in the kitchen area, the hubbub of others trying to communicate in so-called whispers which echoed all around the place, and the general mêlée of folks packing up their beds and bags. Outside, the dozens of cyclists made no effort at all to control their noise. In fact, it seemed that to a man, and woman, they had all decided to test their bicycle bells at one and the same time, creating a percussion of sound that would have graced any major orchestra. Shaking myself out of sleep I wondered if there was some kind of emergency evacuation in place: was the building on fire? Was the whole world on the move, both inside and outside of the albergue? Was there some kind of mass evacuation under way? But as my sleep-befuddled brain cleared I realised it was just two hundred pilgrims gearing up for the day ahead.

On top of all this noise, rain was lashing at the windows; the first real rain, as opposed to the odd spit and spot, that I had encountered since leaving England three weeks ago. In the midst of all this hullaballoo I had no alternative but to get myself together and get back on the trail.

The route out of Ponferrada was depressingly ugly. Inevitable really, as it is virtually encircled by modern day "progress" and quite reminiscent of the suburbs of both the cities of Burgos and Leon.

Walking in grey, persistent rain, wearing my wet weather gear for the first time added to the misery of the start of the day.

However, after little more than a mile the countryside opened up to countless shades of green and stunning views, even through the mist of rain!

To lift my spirits I sang as I walked, racking my memory for every tune sung by Guy Mitchell and romping through She Wears Red Feathers, Poor Little Robin Walking to Missouri, One of the Roving Kind - and Singing the Blues. In no time I was walking on air, fuelled by the music and the wonderful fresh smell of a newly rain-washed world.

The two hundred other pilgrims who had shared the albergue in Ponferrada with me must have all gone off at a cracking pace and left me far behind as once again I was winding my own solitary way, albeit over patches that were sticky and slippery underfoot where it had been churned up by those who had gone before. There were many times when I was glad of my two sticks to keep me upright and on my feet.

Villafranca del Bierzo is one of the prettiest little towns that I have ever seen.

The main square and gardens looked splendid as the rain eased off and the sun broke through the clouds. Outside a building that I took to be the social club or meeting place for pensioners, there stood a magnificent white statue (possibly more than twice life-size) of an elderly couple, a man and a woman, she with a posy of flowers in her hand. It looked as if they were just married. The statue is so big and yet so sweet, I straightaway fell in love with it! The title beneath proclaims

A NUESTROS MAYORES
– a tribute to the older people in the town. I can't imagine such a statue being erected in any town in England and remaining pristine and free from graffiti!

One particular older person in Villafranca, who is a legend in his own time, is a man called Jesus Jato. He is reputed to be almost eighty-years-old and for decades he and his family have dedicated their lives to helping pilgrims. He is the current head of the family who run the refugio Ave Fenix (apparently thus named because the original refugio burnt down!) Jesus Juto is also said to be something of a mystic and spiritual healer, so I decided to stay the night there and maybe soak up some spiritual recharging of my inner being.
As I neared the entrance to the refuge a young woman leaning against the church wall, her face turned towards the sun whilst enjoying a cigarette, beckoned me over. Tilting her head and blowing out a billow of cigarette smoke, speaking almost from the side of her mouth she asked if I intended to spend the night there.
I nodded.
She curled her bottom lip, narrowed her eyes against yet another billow of smoke, and shook her head.
'Not a good place', she said, in heavily accented English.
'Why?' I asked.

She shrugged her shoulders and then began to tell me that the facilities were quite basic, the place was cold and draughty and that there was not enough hot water. She told me that she had stayed there last night and had been most uncomfortable. As it was now after 1.00 p.m. I asked her why she was still there.

She told me she had been exploring the town, waiting for the rain to ease off and that she was now about to have a light snack before walking on to Ruitelan. She ended up by asking if I would like to join her. I said that I too wanted to explore the town, especially the buildings of interest such as the castle, the Parador, and various ancient churches. She stubbed out her cigarette and walked up to the refugio and with a slight twitch of her head encouraged me to follow her. Over her shoulder she told me that if I don't look at the town, I won't miss much!

A wizened old man, none other than Jesus Jato himself, greeted us with a wide smile that revealed a great shortage in the tooth department, and those that remained were distinct shades of yellow, black and brown!

I cast my gaze around and had to agree that the place was not the most palatial that I had seen on my travels.

The young woman pulled two rickety chairs up to a small round table, beckoned me to sit on one and asked if I would like to share a meal with her. I nodded OK, shook myself out of my rucksack and peeled off my wet-weather gear.

We had bread, cheese and tomato with huge mugs of coffee. She told me she was from Belgium and that her name is Barbara. I introduced myself to her and we exchanged a few pleasantries whilst we ate.

Our meal over, she stood up and asked me again if I wanted to walk on with her. I don't know what it was about her but I seemed unable to do anything other than comply with her suggestions. I nodded OK again, but then a shiver immediately ran through my body. What on earth was I thinking about? I had already walked ten or eleven miles and now here I was volunteering to walk another ten. Two or three weeks ago I wouldn't even have considered such a reckless idea. What had happened to my promise to myself to take a "softly, softly approach to travelling"?

This young woman, Barbara, seemed to have bewitched me.

In the little time I had spent in her company I had allowed her to override my innate common sense. She was about 40-odd years younger than me, almost a foot taller and looked reasonably fit in life and limb. Why would I expect to keep pace with her over another ten mile stretch of the Camino?

I needn't have worried – we walked together as one.

It was good for me to have a companion to share thoughts, feelings, hopes and ideas with.

Barbara had planned her itinerary meticulously and she told me about a special place, called O Cebreiro, that she was going to visit the next day. She assured me that we must see it together.

We talked and we walked.

The way led along a steep valley path, through incredibly beautiful and ancient woodlands full of chestnut trees, conifers and holm-oaks. However, the main road often burst into the tranquillity, making the route not only noisy but also extremely dangerous as traffic shot by at alarming speeds. The roadside bits apart, the scenery was quite stunning and the freshness of the air after the rain was a delight to my lungs. Barbara was sure-footed and seemed to know the trail by heart. I felt safe in her company and convinced myself that she was an Angel of Guidance sent to help me on my way, especially as she led me to the most intriguing refugio of my journey so far.

I was really ready to rest when we entered what I assumed to be a tiny, roadside village house. Again, Barbara seemed to know what to expect but I was overwhelmed by the soothing sounds of Gregorian chants and other such music that filtered through the rooms. This refugio was run by two very kindly, gentle men who seemed to me to have leanings towards Buddhism. They shared the chores of running the place and also offered pilgrims homeopathic remedies and Shiatsu massage. So, I could get my spiritual batteries charged today after all!

I spent an hour-and-a-half before supper being massaged with the most heady of perfumed oils and pampered into a virtual stupor. It was a delightful way to relax my tired body and feet and finally ease the last lingering pain from my ankle.

Thank you again - Barbara - for leading me here!

I wrote some postcards to family and friends and walked a kilometre down the road to post them. On the way back I bumped into the young Englishman I had met in Leon – the one who had arrived in the night and had plans to open the "Swinging Cymbal" bar in Berlin.

He told me that today was his birthday, so he was offering bread and wine to every pilgrim he met.

We sat on a low stone wall and he pulled half a French loaf from a plastic carrier-bag, a bottle of red wine and some plastic cups. He broke off a lump of bread for each of us, then poured out a generous splash of wine for me and a tinier one for himself. We spent a pleasant short time together. I wished him many more happy birthdays ahead and the best of luck for his Berlin venture, and he went off to continue his planned walking for that day.

Back at the refugio, rather than it being an irritation I strangely enough found the continuous background music (like meditation, chanting, relaxation) deeply soothing to my soul.

This place was having a profound effect on me.

I felt as though I was moving on to a different spiritual plane.

The feeling was compounded when I noticed a picture of a little girl walking with a guardian angel on the wall above my bed.

Placing my stone from Eastbourne

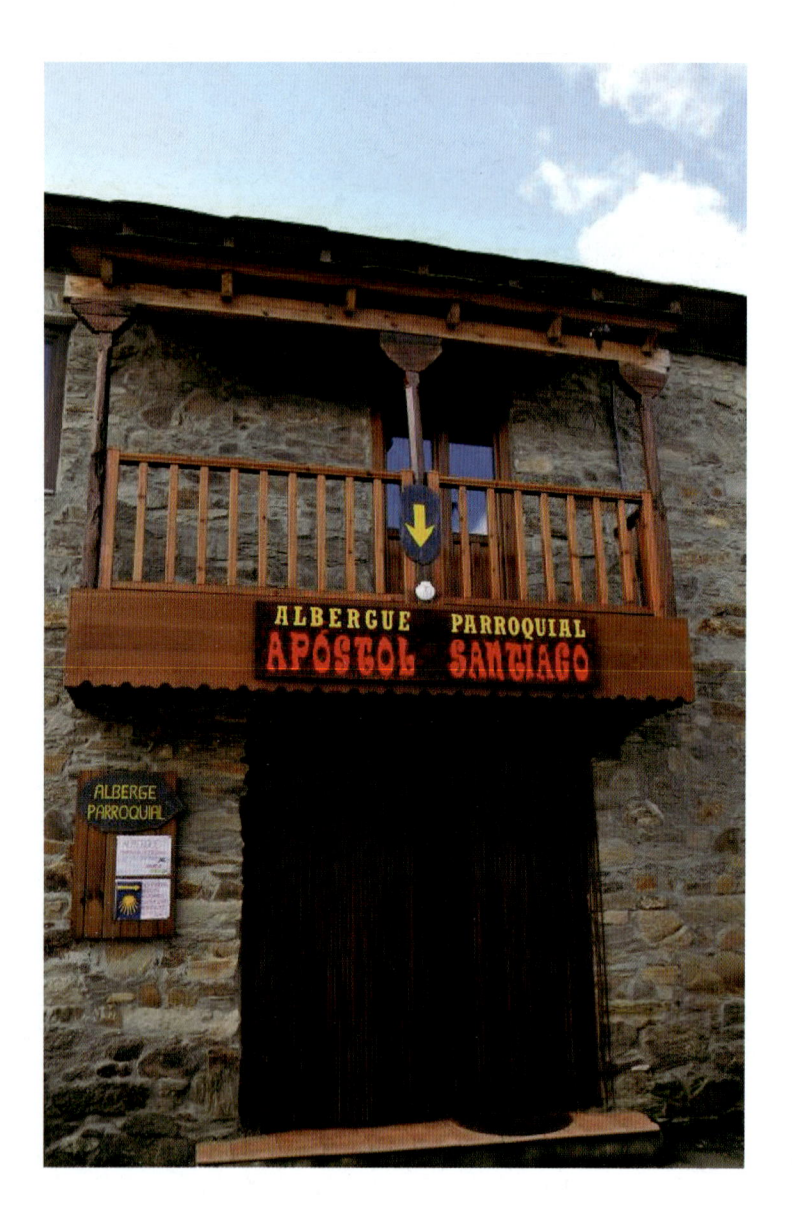

Albergue Acebo

View from mountains above Ponferrada

Almost there and still smiling

Palas de Rei- chilling out

NINTH-PRAYER TO THE APOSTLE SANTIAGO

Oh glorious apostle Santiago, you selected among the first ones! You were the first, among the Apostles, to drink the chalice of the Lord. Oh, happy village of Spain, protected by someone called Patrono! For you the Almighty has done big works, hallelujah.

– *Paternoster, Ave Maria and Glory* –

Bright star of Spain, apostle Santiago, your body rests in peace, your glory survives among us, hallelujah.

– *Pray for us, blessed Santiago* –

– *To be proper to reach the promises of our Lord Jesus Christ* –

Pray: Almighty and eternal God, you that consacrated the first works of the Apostles with the blood of Santiago, make that, by his martyrdom, your Church becomes stiffened and, by his patronage, Spain keeps loyal to Christ until the end of the days.

For Jesus Christ our Lord. Amen.

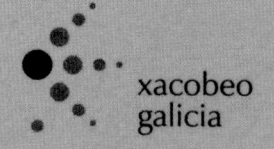

xacobeo
galicia

Prayer card given to me by the Cure of Boente

It wasn't all footslog

Cathedral at Santiago with Jorge

CAPITULUM hujus Almae Apostolicae et Metropolitanae Ecclesiae Compostellanae sigilli Altaris Beati Jacobi Apostoli custos, ut omnibus Fidelibus et Peregrinis ex toto terrarum Orbe, devotionis affectu vel voti causa, ad limina Apostoli Nostri Hispaniarum Patroni ac Tutelaris **SANCTI JACOBI** convenientibus, authenticas visitationis litteras expediat, omnibus et singulis praesentes inspecturis, notum facit: Dnam *Margaritam de Vos* hoc sacratissimum Templum pietatis causa devote visitasse. In quorum fidem praesentes litteras, sigillo ejusdem Sanctae Ecclesiae munitas, ei confero.

Datum Compostellae die 24 mensis Aprilis anno Dni 2009.

My Compostella

Some of the stamps in my Pilgrim passport

RUITELAN to FONFRIA

Friday 17th April 2009 (19th day of walking)

AVE MARIA BEING PLAYED AT DISCO DECIBEL level exploded around the room.
The sound of the music almost blasted me out of my skin. After only two seconds of it I swear that nowhere in the entire house could there have been a body still in its bed. This was a surreal start to the day in anyone's books! Barbara chivvied me along – she had already arranged for our rucksacks to be taken on ahead by car to the albergue at Fonfria, over fifteen miles away. She fussed like a mother hen and had us out of the door and on our way before 6.30 a.m.
From the start, the route was a steady climb along a surfaced road edged with tall trees. The morning was fresh and clear. It had rained during the night and as the trail dipped to cross a sparkling, swiftly flowing river I felt a huge sense of elation and became almost overwhelmed with emotion and gratitude to have Barbara as my

travelling companion; it took all my inner reserves to stop me from bursting into tears of joy.

Soon we were climbing a dauntingly steep track that must have been a couple of miles long, through beautiful woodland floored with ferns and bracken. Even with the help of my two sticks it was all I could do to put one foot in front of the other. It would have been an impossibility with my rucksack on my back. All the while Barbara was giving me gentle, positive encouragement, and I don't think I would have managed this stretch of the Camino without her.

Just when I thought I could go no further we came to a clearing and the tiny village of La Faba, where we stopped for a mid-morning dose of milky coffee, toast and jam. It was a massive relief to sit for a while and ease the searing pain ripping through my calves, buttocks and thighs.

Again, for a moment I really felt I was ready to call a halt to my Camino pilgrimage, but what choice did I have? Should I just turn round and scramble back down to Ruitelan? Barbara seemed to read my thoughts. Her voice was urgent and persistent in my ears.

'We are more than half way up. It will be a shorter task to continue than it would be to go back'

I felt trapped in a dilemma and too weary to think straight, so once again I did as Barbara suggested. I took a deep breath, stood up, straightened back my shoulders and gave her a watery smile as I hobbled towards the door.

As we left the bar I stopped dead in my tracks. My jaw dropped and I blinked in amazement. I felt as if I had been transported to some winter wonderland –

It was snowing . . .

. . . gentle soft flakes, and yet the sun was shining, creating dozens of dancing rainbows.

It was a truly magical sight, which lasted for only five or ten minutes before the sun went behind a cloud and the snowflakes turned to slight and sleety rain.

As we set off once more the trail became murderously steep and slippery underfoot.

We zigzagged our way slowly upwards for another mile or so, although if my legs and feet could talk they would probably profess to have done four or five times that length of track.

Most of the time I was only able to progress in a sideways, crab-like fashion, using my arms and sticks to lever myself along. I was practically at the end of my tether when we reached a wide sweep of grassy slopes. Almost faint with exhaustion I fell in a heap on to the damp, sweet, soft turf. Tears flowed down my cheeks unwanted and unbidden. Barbara sat beside me, she rifled in her pocket and pulled out a bar of fruit and nut chocolate which she snapped in half – one half each. Where the hell did she get it from I wondered, but was too tired to ask? The effect of the chocolate, nuts and fruit was like refuelling an old car on high-octane gas. I slowly wiped my tear-stained face, took a long swig of icy water from my bottle, then struggled back to my feet suitably fortified for the last leg of my assault on O Cebreiro.

We soon passed the boundary stone marking our entry into Galicia; not only was I now on the last part of my mountain climb, but officially also on the very last leg of my journey along the Camino.

A huge sigh of relief escaped my weary lungs as I ambled onwards and finally staggered into the ancient village of oval shaped thatched buildings that is O Cebreiro – a settlement that has sheltered pilgrims for centuries.

I looked back down across the soft green Galician landscape and marvelled at what I had achieved.

However, before I could offer even so much as a silent prayer of thanks, Barbara led me straight to the church. I felt as if I had lost my thinking skills and all freedom of choice. Since I had met her yesterday I had been at her beck and call and had blindly and obediently followed her instructions. Where she had led, I had gladly followed. I know for certain that without her I would never have accomplished my climb to this mountain top, and am positive that I would never have attempted, let alone completed, the last ten miles or so of my walk from Ponferrada to Ruitelan yesterday.

The church was aglow with soft lights and candles. Inner peace swept through me as I made my way towards the altar.

I sat on a front row pew, sure in the knowledge that if I knelt down it would need a fork-lift truck to get me back on my aching legs and feet!

I gave thanks for having the health and strength to get so far on my Camino journey and extra thanks for the help and guidance of Barbara, who had enabled me to achieve an uphill trek of nine kilometres from Ruitelan and a climb of almost 1,300 metres in just under six hours.

I lit several candles for family and friends, put the most delightfully pictorial stamp in my pilgrim passport and followed Barbara to the nearby hostelry.

The bar was crowded with a group of cyclists, young Spanish men who looked to be in their late teens or early twenties. They were happy, boisterous and extremely noisy.

I must have looked wrecked when I entered the room as they all stopped their jovial antics and stared at me in amazement. One of them asked if I had just climbed O Cebreiro. I nodded and flashed them the biggest smile I could muster, which wasn't much, and said, 'Si!' – at which they looked somewhat awestruck.

One brave lad then asked how old I was.

'Soy setenta años,' (I am seventy-years-old) I replied.

They all clapped and cheered and crowded round me, shook my hands, kissed my cheeks and gave me huge hugs.

They insisted on paying for my lunch.

I was overwhelmed by their spontaneity and generosity, which lifted my spirits and energy levels to unprecedented heights.

Barbara sat at the table beside me, beaming happiness to all and sundry.

We had a wonderful lunch from an excellent array of tapas and a glass of red Rioja that was nectar to my lips.

After a large coffee and more hugs and kisses from the cyclists we were back on the trail again; Barbara leading the way of course!

The rain had cleared and a weak sunshine reflected the beauty of the Galician countryside. Raindrops still dripped and sparkled on the trees and shrubs along the route and reminded me of late spring time at home on the Sussex Downs.

Soon, the day seemed to drift into an anti-climax and my walking pace dropped to little more than a dawdle.

Barbara wanted to go ahead and secure a bed space for us at the albergue so I hugged her, waved her off and continued on, locked in my own solitary thoughts.

'Where's your bag?'

A robust question in an accent definitely from the north of England broke into my reverie, and there before me stood an eye-popping example of glorious manhood. He was about forty-years old, six-feet tall and tanned, with dark hair in tight curls cut short above his ears, and his muscular arms were crossed over the most huggable chest I had seen for ages. He had a pair of impish brown eyes that would have any red- blooded woman heading immediately for the bedroom.

He could have walked straight from the pages of a Mills and Boon novel.

Recovering my breath, I asked, 'Where are you from?'

'I asked you first!'

His lovely eyes were dancing and I felt my jaw slacken in lust, followed by a swift intake of breath!

I looked about me. He was standing by the garden gate of a small, round cottage somewhat similar to the buildings in O Cebreiro. The only other building in sight was what looked like a huge black barn on the other side of the road.

'Where am I?' I asked.

'You're in a little place called Fonfria,' he said.

'Well, if that's the albergue . . .', I nodded towards the barn, 'my bag should be in there.'

A cheeky grin creased his face and crinkled his eyes. My throat tightened.

'OK! Your turn now. Where are you from? I asked him again.

He nodded and smiled.

My knees began to buckle.

'Liverpool; and - yep, that is the albergue.'

'Are you a pilgrim? I asked.

'Nope, I live here.' He jerked a thumb nonchalantly back towards the cottage, and I almost gagged as his bicep bulged beneath the sleeve of his tee-shirt.

I shook my head, waved him a swift 'adios' and crossed the road towards the albergue, hardly believing that such a specimen of superb masculinity could live in this wilderness, so far from his homeland. On the other hand, he was such a walking temptation that maybe he was here for his own safety!

My rucksack and Barbara were waiting for me at the bar. This was a really civilised albergue!
I ordered a pot of tea: 'English style please, with milk.'
It was quite a big place, and yet here it was at just after four in the afternoon already milling with people of all nationalities.
A huge German guy joined us at the bar and introduced himself as A.J. He was grey-haired and rather grizzled but had a friendly, chirpy character. He spoke English with a thick Welsh accent that sounded a bit like Tom Jones. He told us that he'd been sent to distant cousins in Wales to learn his English. He was a complete joker and had everyone around us doubled up with laughter as he told story after story in his Welsh/English accent. With my jaws aching from laughter I excused myself and went to make up my bed, shower and change before coming back down to join Barbara for our evening meal.
Back downstairs Barbara was sitting at a table with Enrico from Madrid and Irma from Holland. She beckoned me over to sit with them. I never cease to be amazed by how many pilgrims use English as a common language to share their Camino experiences.
The company was pleasant and relaxed and we all contributed to a meal, some bits bought at the bar, fresh fruit given by Enrico, and bread, ham and salami from Irma.
Just as we were finished eating I noticed that the guy from Liverpool, who I had "flipped" over such a short while ago, was now sitting up there at the bar watching me. I gave him a tiny wave and a smile, so he came over to our table. A.J. the German joined him, and they both pulled up

chairs. He sat beside me and introduced himself to us all as Dean. A.J. led the conversation and there was more hilarity as he talked about things he had seen and done and some of those he had met on his trek so far. Eventually, he asked Dean what had brought him to Fonfria and how he managed to survive so far from civilization. I was interested to hear Dean reply that he owned a string of horses and was a tour guide for long distance, cross country riding holidays. He invited us to look at his home and horses.

Barbara and I decided to stay in the bar and soon others joined us round the table for a quiet time of drinks and general Camino chit-chat, largely about sharing experiences of climbing O Cebriero and the subsequent aches and pains that we all were suffering.

Soon Dean returned to the bar and again pulled up a chair to sit beside me. My heart was beating wildly and I was filled with a mixture of fear, apprehension and excitement. I felt almost like a teenager on a chemically-charged first date and struggled to hide my emotions. Before long it seemed that he and I were the only ones in the bar. He told me that he was divorced, had two children that he rarely saw and how that situation broke his heart. He asked me how I was physically managing the rigours of walking so far each day. I told him about my replacement toe joint, my ankle problems and how I had struggled with my oversized rucksack. It was as if we were old friends. He told me that the surface of the Camino from Fonfria was extremely rough and advised me to walk on the roadside, at least for the next several miles or so. He said that the road ran parallel to the Camino and that I would still be in contact with the spirituality of the trail, but it would most certainly be easier on my feet.

Around nine-o'clock people began to drift off to bed. I went with Barbara and A.J. as we were in nearby bunks and it seemed like the right thing to do, rather than go later and maybe disturb them. Dean wished me goodnight with a Spanish style kiss on each cheek. I was shocked by the intensity of feeling that he communicated in his touch and appalled at my adrenal-charged response. I was glad to retreat to the safety of the dormitory and allow my heart rate to calm down.

FONFRIA to SAMOS

Saturday 18th April 2009 (20th day of walking)

BARBARA SHOOK ME AWAKE at 7.00 a.m. and told me she was about to leave.
She hugged me, wished me luck for the rest of my journey - and was gone. (I never saw her again, have no photograph of her or even know her surname or where she lived in Belgium, but I will never forget her and shall always be grateful to have spent with her the time that I did).
Angela, the hostaleria made a special breakfast for me of toast and puréed fresh tomatoes with hot, strong coffee. She would accept no payment and invited me back, as her guest, whenever I was in Galicia.
I left just after 8.00 a.m. and walked along the road to Triacastela. The smooth surface certainly was easy on my feet and I made good progress; so much so that I allowed myself a coffee break before taking the road to Samos. I sat in a sunny spot outside a roadside café and had fantasies of Dean riding up on a white charger and carrying me off to his castle.

I continued to walk on the roadside and arrived on the outskirts of Samos just before 1.00 p.m. where . . .

. . . I was quite shaken rigid, because standing smiling broadly beside a battered old van and obviously waiting there for me – was none other but Dean.

My heart developed palpitations as he beckoned me over.
'What are you doing here and how did you know I was coming to Samos?'

'Waiting for you, silly. You never said good-bye.' His smile widened. 'In any case, you broadcast to everyone last night that this is where you were coming.'

He moved behind me, eased my rucksack off my back and slung it easily across one shoulder. I hoped he didn't feel me shaking. He put his free arm round my shoulders, pulled me to him in a bear hug and planted a kiss on the top of my head. Again it was as if we were intimate old friends. He guided me into a little restaurant and chose a table in a secluded corner. My nerves abated and common sense kicked in. My body shuddered through an involuntary shiver.

'You've got a nerve, thinking I might be glad to see you.'
He just smiled and shrugged.

This situation seems to have shades of "Shirley Valentine" about it and he must be the Camino Lothario, I thought, easing my chair a little way from his while at the same time chiding myself for having been so vulnerable and gullible last night. He is rather lovely though, said my weak inner voice.

Dean ordered tea for the two of us, going on to tell me that he was on his way to get hay for his horses and just hoped that he might see me again.

'I bet you say that to all the women,' I retorted and screwed up my nose towards him.

He looked visibly hurt and I felt mean for having been so blunt. He took hold of my hand and looked straight into my eyes.

'I know it is madness, but I felt drawn towards you the minute you came plodding down the road, and no, I don't say it to all the women. I am in Spain as it is to recover from female- inflicted pain.'

My heart melted, but I withdrew my hand from his and changed the subject.

'I have heard that a visit to the monastery here is a Camino "must do" so I am going to book in there for tonight, so that I can have a tour of the place and perhaps join the monks for their evening service,' I said, cool and matter of factly.

'Yep,' he nodded. 'It is a treat to see but the albergue part of it is a bit basic.'

'Oh, shame, I had it down as being equal to a Parador!'

The tension lifted and we were back to being relaxed and friendly again.

We sat for a while longer, finishing our tea, then I stood up to go. When Dean lifted my rucksack to help me put it on he spotted my old police whistle that I had been given by my grandfather when I joined the Girl Guides almost sixty years ago. My grandfather had been an A.R.P. (air-raid precaution) warden during the Second World War and had been issued with the whistle as part his equipment. I had been urged to take it with me as its shrill piercing sound would carry far and bring help if ever I was in difficulty. The whistle was tied with string to a strap on my rucksack within easy reach in any emergency. I undid it with a shrug and told Dean he could have it as a reminder of me. I was trying to untie the string, but he held my hand and stopped me.

'I should like to keep the piece of string too, if I may,' he said, his eyes gazing deeply into mine.

Oh, blow; my throat tightened and my heart melted again. It was all I could do to remain focused and steady. My head and heart started a serious discussion - was he a practiced womaniser, or was he serious? My head won. I gave him the whistle, with the string attached, shrugged into my rucksack and made to walk away, but he clasped me for one last hug. I remained strong, stepped back, smiled and pulled a wry face. I

waved goodbye, turned and walked across the road and on to the monastery.

With mixed feelings and emotions swirling around in my head I reached the entrance to the albergue part of the monastery only to discover that it was closed for lunch. There was a restaurant opposite so I opted for a solitary meal and a little emotional respite.

I still felt really tired and drained when the doors to the albergue were finally opened. I just dumped my rucksack beside my allotted bunk, took off my boots, fell onto the bed and was asleep in seconds.

The clattering of a large group of pilgrims, in cheerful good spirits woke me with a start. The tour of the monastery was about to begin. I felt so low in spirits and sluggish that I decided to give it a miss, but I did go to the evening service where about ten or twelve monks gathered to sing vespers. The singing was divine but the monks were a motley bunch. One of them was very tall and lean with mad bulging eyes. He may well have had problems with his thyroid but he looked slightly unhinged to me. The rest of them were tiny roly-poly creatures, all of whom looked to be extremely old and definitely of another world!

Back in the dormitory the temperature had dropped dramatically. I managed to find four extra blankets but couldn't get warm or comfortable enough to settle down to sleep. There were two people sharing one sleeping bag in the bunk next to me, and when they began making quiet, gentle love I retreated into slumber and left them to it.

SAMOS to PORTOMARIN

Sunday 19th April 2009 (21st day of walking)

THE HOSPITALERO CAME BREEZING IN at 7.00 a.m. and switched on all the lights.
He was bright and bustly and stopped just short of blowing reveille to get us all out of bed.
I was on the road by 7.45 a.m.
My spirits were decidedly low and matched the misty, cloudy weather. I stayed on the road rather than risk the uneven surface of the Camino trail, and arrived in Sarria before 10.00 a.m.
The town was virtually deserted with hardly a soul in sight.
It is a depressing sort of place, just blocks of nondescript modern-style buildings.
I walked straight on until I came to a new road system which rose steeply and left the town behind. By midday the sun broke through the clouds and the temperature began to soar. I was tired, very hot and desperate for a

shady spot to rest a while, when a stroke of luck or
another Camino miracle occurred.

A minibus, full of jolly Spaniards pulled up to a halt
beside me.

The driver swung open his door and greeted me with a
cheery, 'Buenos dias'.

Quite out of breath, I just managed to nod in response.
Soon several of the passengers clambered out of the bus
and gathered around me. They were largely middle-aged
or older men and women in all shapes and sizes. They told
me that they were a group of "friends of the Camino"
committed to helping pilgrims, and insisted in taking me
up to the top of the hill in their bus.

Who was I to argue?

We made a "comfort stop" at a wayside restaurant where
a selection of tapas and drinks were ordered and enjoyed
around a long table under the shade of a large umbrella,
where in a mix of broken English and simple Spanish this
merry group of friends related to me a little of the history
of Portomarin.

As far as I could gather, before a new reservoir was built
there the old town was dismantled brick-by-brick and
rebuilt some way up the hill in its present position.

From there I thanked them for their friendship and
hospitality and carried on to the municipal refugio.

The weather was beautifully warm and sunny.

It was still only four-o'clock in the afternoon so I did some
washing and chatted to a small group of pilgrims from
several different countries, all of them again using English
as a communal language.

I was still feeling disturbed by my encounter with Dean
and couldn't fully engage with the other pilgrims, so as
soon as my washing was dry I re-packed my bag ready for

the next stage of my trek, ever conscious that I was now only days away from Santiago.

I went to bed early and was asleep almost as soon as my head touched the pillow.

PORTOMARIN to PALAS DE REI

Monday 20th April 2009 (22nd day of walking)

A HIVE OF ACTIVITY . . . with pilgrims shuffling to bathrooms, packing their bags, "whispering" to companions or banging doors behind them, had me awake and out of bed by 6.30 a.m.

After a quick drink of water, a brief wash and hurried stowing of my bedroll, I was ready for the road by seven. As I was leaving, a Scandinavian chap kindly adjusted all the straps on my rucksack which made it surprisingly much easier for me to carry. Why-oh-why hadn't this happened on Day One?

The morning was cool and fresh and just a little misty. A young German guy asked if he could walk with me for a while because he wanted to practise his English. He told me he was from Oberammergau, in southwest Germany's Bavarian Alps. He was excited by the thought of taking part in their world famous Passion play, which happens only every ten years, and was due to take place again next year. He said that almost everyone in the town had a part to play. He was hoping for a major role for himself, but first would have to grow a beard and not have a haircut for several months.

He was a tall, athletic young man with ice blue eyes and blond hair and an open, honest face. He had a warmth to his demeanour which was kind and friendly. He told me that as part of his national service he was training to be a nurse.

He walked with me for almost three hours, which must have been a trial for him, matching his long legs to my tiny strides.

It felt good to be back on the Camino trail again as opposed to the paved streets, and I enjoyed being amongst the beauty of the Galician countryside.

I walked almost effortlessly, barely noticing the kilometres which I had covered, happy to be able to enjoy the company and enthusiasm of my young companion.

The track was a steady climb, and by the time we reached Gonzar we were both ready for breakfast.

I had two fried eggs with ham and fresh bread and a glass of ice-cold beer.

We were joined by two lovely Irish women, both in their late thirties or early forties and full of charm and banter. I think the young lad was rather overwhelmed by the vivacity of the women and their chirpy conversation.

He bade me a very polite goodbye and was gone from sight in no time.

Ann-Marie told me that she worked in the prison service in Ireland and was walking the Camino during an extended period of leave in order to bring some peace and a sense of quiet spirituality back into her life.

Carmella didn't say much about her personal life, perhaps because she was enjoying the lavish breakfast she was tucking into with such relish.

We three women were just about to set off walking together when three portly, middle-aged Spanish women arrived and encouraged us to join them.

They were a really jolly trio.

They told us they were sisters from Madrid and had taken a few days away from their families to walk the last hundred kilometres of the Camino as an offering of thanks for the good lives they all shared.

Before long they began to sing songs, all about the Camino, at the tops of their lungs and with huge depths of feeling, which was quite infectious, and although we didn't know the words we were soon all smiling broadly and humming along with the tunes.

At Ventas de Naron we stopped for some cooling drinks and met another group of very friendly pilgrims.

The Spanish women lingered only briefly before continuing on their merry musical way and the two Irish women soon followed them.

I stayed longer and discovered that the new group were a man, who introduced himself as Alan, and his wife – Maureen, from a small town near Toronto, in Canada.

Their accompanying friend, Carmen, was from Valencia. Immediately I felt a strong empathy towards these three people, and that it would be good for me to walk with them for a while.

They were very warm and friendly and welcomed me into their company.

As we walked they soon began to share their reasons why they were doing the Camino together.

They had met a few years ago, when Alan and Maureen had been walking from St-Jean-Pied-de-Port to Santiago and Carmen was walking with her husband during Holy Week of that year.

They had become firm friends during that week and had stayed in touch ever since.

Carmen and her husband had continued to walk part of the Camino together each Holy Week until last year, when they had reached Ponferrada.

Unfortunately, just before Christmas Carmen's husband had lost his job and plunged into a deep depression.

Money worries plagued him and he lost all hope until – in final desperation - he had taken his own life.

Carmen had been and was still devastated by this, but was determined to walk the last two hundred kilometres of the Camino in her husband's memory.

In an unprecedented act of friendship Maureen and Alan had volunteered to come from Canada to walk with her, to comfort and support her whenever she needed them.

I found their story deeply moving, especially when I was walking alone for a time with Carmen and she told me in her halting English that in all her life her husband had been the only person who had ever said they loved her.

We arrived at Palas de Rei by mid-afternoon and booked into the municipal albergue.

This was a large, fairly dilapidated house in the town centre, stuffed with as many bunks as was humanly possible to cram into rooms, with hardly a breathing space between them.

The windows of the shower and toilet areas looked straight on to the street, giving passers-by a not very appetizing sideshow as weary pilgrims of assorted shapes and sizes performed their ablutions.

The shower curtain was hanging in shreds and virtually useless.

Ever the gentleman, Alan held up his huge waterproof poncho to spare the blushes of us women as we showered, one after the other, in water that became ever cooler, so that by the time poor Alan got in his shower was icy cold. Although the trail had been largely uphill, I had met such a diverse group of really interesting people I had barely noticed the climb or the miles we had covered, and after my shower felt quite energised and refreshed – apart from having what felt like the beginning of a sore throat.

Maureen, Alan, Carmen and I sat on the sunny terrace of the bar opposite the albergue where we were soon joined by a couple of Spanish pilgrims and a jolly Dutch woman. I had a triple-sized glass of freshly squeezed orange juice laced with a Spanish-sized shot of brandy - purely medicinal, you understand - to ease my sore throat! We spent a happy hour chatting and sharing Camino experiences before going off to a nearby restaurant for our evening meal.

The meal was pure pilgrim food, pasta and salads and lots of local wines. We laughed a great deal together (maybe the result of the wines!) and again the communal language was English. No wonder we British, as a nation, are rubbish at languages; we don't even have to try while the whole rest of the world strives to speak some version or other of our native tongue.

By the time I tumbled into my bunk I was relaxed and ready for sleep, but three young Australian women came back late from their revels and shook my bed almost to bits as they jostled and joked with each other before finally dropping off to sleep themselves, by which time I was wide awake again. In desperation, I took a sleeping pill and soon joined them in the "land of Nod".

PALAS DE REI to MELIDE

Tuesday 21st April 2009 (23rd day of walking)

I AWOKE WITH A SPLITTING HEADACHE and a raw, sore throat.
The boisterous Australian girls shook the place back to life and their raucous humour had most of the other pilgrims either smiling or grimacing.
I just wanted to go back to sleep.
Maureen, Alan and Carmen were already packing their bags, so I pulled myself together and managed to set off with them before 7.00 a.m.
We were joined by a tiny Spanish couple, Luis and Isabel, who had been with us for dinner the night before.
I was operating on auto-pilot and really struggling, feeling decidedly unwell.
Alan suggested that we stop at San Xulian for breakfast, where we arrived in the middle of an argument between the hospitalero and a group of German pilgrims disputing items on their bill. They refused to pay the full amount

and we heard the angry hostalero telephone several other albergues to alert them of the problems he had had.

Luis and Isabel were a joy to be with.

Both aged about sixty and newly retired, they exuded a sense of calm contentment and well-being. It was easy to be in their company. They too came from Valencia and it turned out they lived fairly near to Carmen: almost as though they sensed her need they each stayed very close to her.

I had a pint of freshly squeezed orange juice – an overload of Vitamin-C to fight whatever was attacking my head and throat, with another brandy chaser to act as an antibiotic and anaesthetic - as well as a couple of large milky coffees, toast and jam to lift me out of the lethargy that was dogging my mood.

The day was rapidly warming and the effect of the heat and the heady smell from the Eucalyptus trees lining the trail soon cleared my headache, but my sore throat stubbornly refused to be soothed.

We decided to stop in Melide for the night, which would leave us only fifty-six kilometres to travel to Santiago.

Alan was our self-appointed route master and he planned for us to arrive in Santiago soon after midday on Friday, in order to be sure of a bed in an albergue or hotel.

Melide was buzzing with pilgrims, and even though it was only a little after one p.m. the albergues were rapidly filling.

After leaving our bags at the albergue we all headed for Pulperia Ezequiel.

This, so the guide books say, is a world famous place to eat the Galician speciality of spiced octopus in wine, served on wooden platters and accompanied by freshly baked bread and white Ribeiro wine – another speciality of Galicia.

The restaurant was absolutely packed with enthusiastic pilgrims all eager to taste the pulpo. I am afraid that, at the last minute, I decided against the octopus, and had a plate of prawns instead. (I did get a stamp in my pilgrim's passport though!)

Those who did eat it were full of its praise.

Each to his (or her) own, I say!

We sat at long trestle tables and a tall, thin, bespectacled man came and joined us. He introduced himself as Jorge and told us he was twenty-nine years-old and from Madrid. He said he was walking the last hundred kilometres of the Camino before entering the seminary, where he intended to take holy orders. His aim was eventually to work with under-privileged children in South America. He was very interesting and as the Italians say, most "simpatico".

Again, I had to marvel at the way fellow pilgrims so readily confide their innermost details to each other.

Back at the albergue I had a shower and did a little bit of washing. I had no time to rest because Alan, Maureen, Carmen, Luis and Isobel had invited me to join them for a look around the town and then on to a pizzeria for supper. I didn't really feel up to it, my throat still feeling quite sore, but I went along anyway because I enjoyed being in their company.

We arrived at the church of Santa Maria only to find it locked and no sign to say if or where there was a key-keeper.

Just as we were about to walk away the priest arrived, with Jorge, but they had an appointment together somewhere and were in a hurry. I was disappointed not to get a stamp from the church, but the old priest wrote a message for me, which roughly translated is - Look for

Christ. When you find him, love him much to be relatively happy in this life and again in heaven:
Andres Geurevo – Cure de Boente.
My dear son, Michael, had sent a text message to my mobile phone telling me he had booked me a room in the Parador, in Santiago, for Friday, Saturday and Sunday - and a flight home from A Coruna to Heathrow on Monday.
The end is definitely in sight now.

MELIDE to ARZUA

Wednesday 22nd April 2009 (24th day of walking)

I SLEPT LONG AND LATE - only waking in time to say goodbye to Alan and co but promising to see them later in the day.
The weather had been kind to me for almost four weeks, cool, mostly dry and sunny, but today it felt decidedly warmer, like early summer in England.
I set off soon after 8.00 a.m. and walked eight kilometres before taking a break.
By ten o'clock the temperature was well up into the eighties. I was baking in my heavy sweater so changed into a lightweight top.
The bar-keeper was a real sweetie.
He said that because I had let my coffee go cold whilst I was changing, he would make me a fresh one – free of charge, and when I was half way through that he topped it up for me with a local cream liqueur.
How's that for service?

After leaving the bar I walked alone and at an easy pace for a while. Several people passed me, but mostly it was just me with my thoughts in quiet meditation.

The first albergue I came to in Arzua was the "Don Quijote".

It was big, it was new, and it looked relatively clean and inviting, but most of all it was open, even though it was still before one p.m.

I checked in, dumped my bags, then went and sat outside the bar next door where I ordered two fried eggs, ham and bread and a pint of beer.

Before my order came, Jorge arrived and decided to join me, which was lovely – even better he paid for my meal and wouldn't take no for an answer.

The sore throat I've had for the last few days now seems to have turned into a cold and attacked my sinuses.

Feeling really rough I slept for a couple of hours in the afternoon. When I woke I had a pint of camomile tea and two Ibuprofen and sat in the sun for a while.

Once the medication kicked in I felt a bit better so I showered and changed and walked down to the municipal albergue to meet with Carmen, Alan and Maureen. We went for a meal together, in a bar opposite my albergue, and it was truly Spanish and truly tasty.

ARZUA to ARCA

Thursday 23rd April 2009 (25th day of walking)

I DIDN'T SLEEP WELL – I coughed and coughed and coughed all night long.
I left just after 6.00 a.m. and met with Maureen, Alan and Carmen, who had planned an early start.
They wanted to cover as many miles as possible before the day became too hot for walking.
We had travelled more than ten kilometres before ten o'clock, so we stopped for cheese on toast and coffee, then pushed straight on.
I lagged a little way behind the group, lost in my own thoughts until I arrived at the tiny hamlet of Santa Irena.
It knocked the breath from my body and stopped me in my tracks.
My sister Irene died on the 3rd of March 1983.
She was only 37-years-old.
Over the intervening years the tangled emotions of loss, anger and unresolved sibling rivalries have plagued and agitated my mind.

During these weeks of walking the Camino Irene had flitted in and out of my consciousness, resulting in many silent tears and periods of extreme frustration, of deep feelings of remorse and anguish. Too late, I often thought, to right the many wrongs, on both our parts.

My biggest difficulty was dealing with the still raw feelings of anger and sense of betrayal that I held towards both her and my then husband because of the long-term, secret sexual relationship they had shared.

When I had finally discovered this my emotions towards them both were volcanic, but had to be contained because my sister was then already dead.

Now here I was in 2009, twenty-six years after her death, foot-weary, blistered, with a head cold and persistent cough, heavily laden and at my lowest ebb, but with only twenty-four kilometres to go to Santiago, and I stumbled into Santa Irena – St. Irene.

With a tightness in my chest and throat that made breathing intensely difficult, I gingerly approached the tiny grotto set into the garden wall of the albergue. In this remote and overgrown garden heavenly scents of orange blossom and jasmine filled the air as unbidden tears ran down my cheeks.

Dropping my rucksack and walking sticks I knelt before the shrine, and following the habits of a Catholic lifetime dipped my fingers into the Holy Water.

'In the name of the Father, the Son and the Holy Ghost', I whispered, then silently asked for help and forgiveness.

I had no idea how long I had knelt there whilst the memories and emotions swirled and surfaced, dipped and dived, returned and revolved. I only know that when I finally stood, emotionally drained but with a heart full of love for my sister and remembrances of all the happy childhood times we had shared, a feeling of peace and contentment washed over me. The contaminations that had blighted our adult relationship were finally gone and I now knew would never return. The relief was tangible and I am sure that when I lifted my rucksack it was decidedly lighter.

I arrived at the albergue rather later than the others, but it was still only mid-afternoon. I had covered only twenty-one kilometres in over seven hours – a snail's pace really, but no more than I could have managed physically or emotionally.

To crown it all I had developed another big blister on the ball of my bad foot. The times that I had felt like giving up on the Camino were never as severe as I felt right now. However, with only one day to go I just had to summon up my last reserves of strength and willpower to get me over this final hurdle.

Once signed in to the refugio I rested a while then went for a light snack meal, and promptly threw it up again, so went back to bed.

Jorge came to visit me at about six o'clock and said that he would come back after he had been to mass. His bedside manner was wonderfully comforting. I told him that I thought he would make a lovely priest.

Carmen came and sat beside me for a while. She held and stroked my hand, which moved me to tears. She gave me a little prayer card, which in English read:-

Hope is my road – victory is my destiny.

I don't know where she got it from, but I shall treasure it for ever.

I got up before Jorge returned and we all shared tapas (well I stuck to dried bread and water!) Jorge had organised for out baggage to be taken to Santiago in a taxi the next morning and dropped off at the Parador for me and the refugio for the others. This was really good news. I felt that I could manage the last twenty-odd kilometres much more readily without having to carry my heavy load.

ARCA to SANTIAGO DE COMPOSTELA

Friday 24th April 2009 (26th day of walking)

I SPENT ANOTHER VIRTUALLY SLEEPLESS NIGHT coughing so much that I gave up all thought of sleeping. I stood looking out of the window for ages, marvelling at the blue-black sky and searching for constellations that I had discovered during my time as a Girl Guide so long ago.
The hillside opposite was thick with pine trees.
I opened the window the merest crack to enjoy their delightful scent on the cool night air. This had a soothing effect on my sinuses and lungs.
When dawn began to break I watched the world change from shades of blue to rosy pinks, and marvelled at the birth of another new day.
As I dressed and packed my bags, so the stirrings of other pilgrims roused the dormitory back to life.
It was deeply satisfying for me to have been accepted as part of the little "family" group that was Carmen and co. I

felt truly cherished and looked after. I wondered if this was more work of the angels of the Camino, and think that it probably was!

We left our bags with Jorge at the designated "drop off" place and set off at a fairly cracking pace.

After about ten kilometres the rain began to drizzle down, so we stopped for coffee and toast and put on our wet-weather gear before walking on.

Whilst we were doing this Jorge caught up with us and we all walked together to Monte del Gozo (Mount of Joy).

This place looked like a grotesque and massive military establishment. Jorge told us there were three-thousand pilgrim bed spaces there, and I fully believed him!

We had lunch together in the huge restaurant, which reminded me of a third-rate British holiday camp of the 1950s. The food seemed to be from that era too!

Jorge planned to spend the night there, so we said our good-byes and promised to meet at the Cathedral next morning for the Pilgrim Mass at 12 noon.

The weather had dried up so we stowed our cagoules and walked the remaining two or three miles through the suburbs of Santiago and on in to the Cathedral Square.

I found this all a bit of an anti-climax.

The place was thronged with pilgrims and we met many people who we had briefly shared time with along our way. There were big hugs, hallos and photo sessions galore going on, and somehow a huge group of us ended up in a restaurant sharing a very noisy lunch. I could have done without this but just seemed unable to stop myself from being swept along by the overwhelming happiness and sense of achievement emanating from the crowds.

After lunch I went with Alan, Maureen and Carmen to present our pilgrim passports for verification and be presented with our Compostelas.

I straightaway had mine photocopied and had both laminated.

It was then, and only then, that an overwhelming sense of relief and achievement flooded through me.

We went en masse into the Cathedral to give thanks for our safe deliverance and to marvel at the splendour of this most sacred of sacred places. We followed the age-old traditions of kissing the foot of the stone statue of St. James, and placing our hands on the stone pillar beneath, where a hand-shaped groove had been worn into the stone by countless thousands of pilgrims before us, and then finally we joined the queue shuffling its way to climb the steps at the back of the altar to embrace the statue of the apostle.

Once these rituals were over I felt totally elated and invited Alan, Maureen, Carmen, Luis and Isabel to join me in my room, in the Parador, for a celebratory drink. I am not sure what the hotel receptionist thought when we bunch of bedraggled pilgrims crossed the gleaming marble threshold of a place that is about as far removed from a pilgrim refugio as it is possible to be.

There were flowers, a bottle of champagne on ice and a tarte de Santiago awaiting us in my room, all courtesy of my lovely son - Michael.

Carmen's first thought was for a shower in a clean and functional bathroom with thick, warm towels on which to dry herself. The others followed like termites, all sampling the luxury soaps, shampoos and other toiletries that were on hand, and one after another each of them emerged pink and clean as a bunch of little cherubs.

Alan opened the champagne, Maureen cut the tarte and soon we were all congratulating and toasting each other on a job well done and enjoying the cake and wine.

When they'd all departed and I was finally left alone, I dropped into a really low mood, feeling . . . what was it all for! I had another glass of champagne and rang for room service to take away all the used towels, asking them to bring me a fresh supply, as well as toiletries and other items that my Camino friends had used or taken with them as souvenirs!

After a long and luxurious bath, bubbled up to my neck in perfumed water, I collapsed into a deep and wonderfully refreshing sleep on a bed of unbelievable comfort which was such an indescribable pleasure after so many nights spent on rattling old iron bunks trapped inside my rapidly deteriorating sleeping bag!

I went down to the dining room, but the solemn sedateness, its perfectly correct waiters and the rich food were more than I could handle after more than a month of "roughing it" on the pilgrim trail, eating largely basic pilgrim food, often in grim, unhygienic and unpleasant places, so that all I could do now was pick at my food – much to the annoyance of the pompous head waiter who tried to make me feel unworthy of his establishment. In my best Spanish I told him that I was too tired to eat but he was welcome to come and watch me do justice to my breakfast next morning.

I liked to think he looked suitably abashed.

Perhaps it was just a disdainful sniff.

SANTIAGO DE COMPOSTELA

Saturday 25th April 2009 (26th day of walking)

I SLEPT LONG AND DEEPLY, cocooned in luxury, enjoyed a delicious breakfast (without sight or sound of the previous night's supercilious head waiter) then took a taxi to the nearest Corte Ingles.
My first priority was to buy some new, un-pilgrim-like clothes, a bottle of my favourite perfume and some cosmetics.
 Shopping complete, I took a taxi back to the Parador, only to find Jorge frantically looking for me, so that I could be in my seat in the Cathedral early and not miss a single second of the pilgrim mass.
When we got there it was to find that Alan, Maureen, Carmen, Luis and Isabel had made sure of a good place from which to view the proceedings, and they shuffled up to allow Jorge and me to join them.
What followed was one of the most overwhelming and emotional experiences of my entire life. A nun, with the

voice of an angel, that echoed around the cathedral and made the hairs on the back of my neck stand on end, sang an introductory hymn.

There was then a roll call of the home-town names of all the pilgrims who had completed their pilgrimage the previous day. I nearly burst with pride when they mentioned my town, Eastbourne.

During the mass the famous Botafumeiro was swung into place by eight monks. This is an enormous censer that hangs from the roof of the Cathedral on long thick ropes with which the monks swing it back and forth in dramatic fashion across the front of the altar, with it dispensing thick clouds of incense accompanied by the inspiring chords of booming organ music. The whole procedure is deeply moving.

No sooner was the mass over than I found myself being enveloped in an enormous bear hug. It was Sara, the young woman I had met on Palm Sunday in Villabilla, just outside Burgos. She was with her boyfriend who had flown down from Sweden to join her, and they had pledged to marry just as soon as possible. Sara assured me that she had cleared away all the demons from her traumatic childhood and was sure that she could make a better effort at marriage and parenthood than her parents had. We gave each other another emotional hug, and then she was gone – off to start her new young life.

Carmen, Luis and Isabel were travelling back to Valencia together, and they gave us all warm wishes and Spanish style kisses of goodbye. All of us were in floods of tears and promising to keep in touch with each other.

All along my journey on the Camino I had carried with me a tiny leather-bound copy of the New Testament that I had been given as a prize from a church group, some fifty-six years ago. I gave this to Jorge and wished him luck in his future ministries. Another very emotional farewell ensued. Finally there was just Alan, Maureen and me, but while we were deciding where to go for lunch we were accosted by Anne-Marie and Carmella, the two happy–go–lucky women from Ireland, who decided to join us.

As we left the Cathedral we bumped into Carol, Gaby and Dan, and a few other pilgrims whom we had all encountered along the way. In all we ended up as a party almost twenty strong and shared a jolly lunch together, made even more enjoyable when A.J., our German who spoke Welsh-accented English joined us and regaled us with even more of his side-splitting stories. This was, undoubtedly, one of the happiest and most memorable days of my life.

I planned to travel to Finistere by bus the next day, and was delighted when Maureen and Alan told me that they too were going there. We agreed to meet at the bus station at ten a.m. next morning to make an early start.

I dressed for dinner in the new clothes I had bought in Corte Ingles, and took great care with my make-up before facing the opulent dining room of the Parador on my own. The waiters were friendly, but I didn't fancy anything on the menu so asked the chef to cook me a little roast lamb. When I got my bill I had been charged an extra twenty-four euros for this, on top of the price of the meal that I didn't have! What a nerve!

TO FINISTERRE

Sunday 26th April 2009

IN MEDIEVAL TIMES Finisterre was considered to be the end of the world.
It has long been a tradition for some modern day pilgrims to travel there, either to walk the 89 kilometres or take a two-and-a half-hour bus ride.
Once at the Atlantic they strip off their pilgrim clothes, bathe naked, and then put on new, or at least clean clothes. Some even go so far as to burn their worn out pilgrim gear on the beaches.
I just wanted to visit Finisterre. - as a fitting way to finish my journey.
Alan and Maureen were waiting for me at the bus station and we quickly boarded the rickety old bus that would take us on the twisting mountain route to the coast.
The smells of stale tobacco smoke, unwashed bodies and diesel fumes were quite overpowering and after only a few minutes I began to feel queasy.
Soon, motion sickness agitated my body.

Luckily the driver was quick enough to stop in time for me to get out and throw up my breakfast into a nearby hedge. Having spent several weeks walking in the fresh air, being trapped in the bus I was overwhelmed by the waves of fetid smells swirling around, making me nauseous and decidedly fragile, so I sat near the door and twice more had to get out to throw up before we reached Finisterre. It was an enormous relief to finally get off the bus and fill my lungs with the bracing freshness of the salty sea air and wonder at the stunning beauty of the Galician coast line. I felt rather weak and wobbly as I slowly walked for two kilometres or so, up the steadily climbing road to the lighthouse at the top of the cliffs.

As I passed the church I heard the glorious sounds of the congregation singing their praises to their God. I quietly entered and sat on a back-row pew. By the number of young people around I think it must have been a children's mass, or family service. Whatever it was I enjoyed a beautifully calming, tranquil experience.

When we emerged from the church's cool, dark splendour the sun was warm and bright. Family groups walked into the little cemetery opposite to pay their respects to their departed loved ones. It was a deeply moving experience as I watched the reverence and respect paid by even the youngest of family members.

Later, I sat beside the lighthouse with Maureen and Alan for a moment of our own individual, quiet contemplation before we made our way down to the beach. We didn't venture into the water (or take off our clothes) but it felt like a completion, an ending, and the perfect way to offer up thanks for our safe deliverance from our Camino travails.

Even though I had had nothing more than sips of water all day, I still had to ask the bus driver to stop on the way back.

The first time, in a quiet country town, the sight of an old woman rushing from the bus and heaving and retching into the shrubs beside the bus stop sent a group of teenagers, all dressed up and primped for their Sunday evening out, screaming and scattering far and wide. When I arrived back in Santiago I took off my vomit-stained jacket and put it in a rubbish bin.

This was definitely the end of my journey.

EPILOGUE

WHAT DID I GAIN FROM MY CAMINO EXPERIENCE?
This can best be described in terms of mind, soul and body.

MIND
I have struggled through many difficulties and traumas from my early life and feel that I have come through many changes. Those people in my life from whom I have been estranged, I have finally let go. I have reasoned that even if they are family or blood relatives they are not the kind of people that I would want to be friends with or even to pass the time of day. Now they are gone from my life. However, if they ever wish to be part of my life again then they must show contrition for past behaviours and change their ways and attitudes. This is a wonderfully liberating feeling for me.

SOUL
The condition of my soul is strictly between me and my God. However, I have had enough uplifting, heart-warming and frankly deeply spiritual experiences along the Camino for me to believe that He is still on my side.

BODY
I didn't lose any weight, but my bum is more pert, my thighs more taut - and my tummy is definitely tighter.

My boobs are still sliding south, but then that's another story . . .!